D0368761

The Library Administration Series

Lowell A. Martin, General Editor

1. Alex Ladenson, *Library Law and Legislation in the United States,* 1982
2. R. Kathleen Molz, *Library Planning and Policy Making,* 1990
3. Donald J. Sager, *Participatory Management in Libraries,* 1982
5. Lowell A. Martin, *Organizational Structure of Libraries,* 1984
6. Norman Stevens, *Communication Throughout Libraries,* 1983
8. Ann E. Prentice, *Financial Planning for Libraries,* 1983
9. Raymond M. Holt, *Planning Library Buildings and Facilities: From Concept to Completion,* 1989
10. Cosette Kies, *Marketing and Public Relations for Libraries,* 1987
11. Lowell A. Martin, *Library Personnel Administration,* 1994

Library Personnel Administration

by
LOWELL A. MARTIN

The Library Administration Series, No. 11

The Scarecrow Press, Inc.
Metuchen, N.J., & London
1994

British Library Cataloguing-in-Publication data available

Library of Congress Cataloguing-in-Publication Data

Martin, Lowell Arthur, 1912–
　　Library personnel administration / by Lowell A. Martin.
　　　　p.　cm. — (The Library administration series ; no. 11)
　　Includes bibliographical references and index.
　　ISBN 0-8108-2839-1 (alk. paper)
　　1. Library personnel management—United States.
I. Title.　II. Series: Scarecrow library administration series ; no. 11.
Z682.2.U5M36　1994
023′.9—dc20　　　　　　　　　　　　　　　　94-6569

CONTENTS

LIST OF FIGURES

PREFACE

The Library Administration series of Scarecrow Press has treated various aspects of management, from the Legal Basis of Library Service to Public Relations and Marketing, from Organization to Finance, from Communication to Planning.

But until now there has been a serious gap in the lack of a volume on Personnel. The present treatment is aimed to fill this gap.

Personnel is the fulcrum around which administration revolves, the foundation on which service is built. It all comes down to human beings. Not objectives. Not organization. Not even money.

People are what count. Get skill and morale and work will get done. Get commitment and enthusiasm and goals will be achieved.

Of course, there are interrelations among the various facets of administration. How can you get good people unless you have money? How can you get production if you don't have organization? How can you adjust to change unless you have resources?

But if somehow the people are there, other attributes will follow. Committed staff will create objectives. Dedicated personnel will fashion an organization. Skillful workers will product just out of a sense of pride. Together they will even find ways to increase the budget.

This volume covers the various aspects of personnel administration as they apply to libraries. The psychological basis of human relations is reviewed first. Organizing a personnel structure is treated, resulting in a position classification plan, a career sequence and a salary scale. Then recruitment, selection and orientation are discussed. Evaluation of personnel is given attention. The legal considerations that apply are summarized. Finally, a look ahead is presented in a chapter on the future of personnel administration.

All to the end of the library that serves effectively today and the library that can change to meet new challenges in the onset of the 21st Century.

Lowell A. Martin
Ticonderoga, New York
September 15, 1993

1. INTRODUCTION

There are no easy formulas or panaceas in personnel administration. People differ beyond what even the most observant person would suspect. Employees come with different tolerances as to what they will accept, with different hang-ups. Some are looking for a career, others just want a paycheck. Some want to participate in staff discussion and in the making of decisions, while others don't want to be bothered. Some need regular encouragement and counseling, others are self-motivated.

In general it is better to have staff who want to be involved, who have ideas and suggestions. Usually they are prepared to make an extra effort once they feel they have been heard. But these are not necessarily the easiest employees for administrators to supervise. Staff members who are less involved are more complacent and less inclined to raise objections. Managers who want a soft spot would do well to pick easy-going employees who are satisfied with their jobs. But this is also a sure way to build a less-than-adequate library, an agency not going the extra step to provide service, an agency that will resist change. If the workers are just floating, the enterprise itself will be dead in the water.

Get the best, the committed, the motivated. But be aware that this will not necessarily make for smooth and easy administration. With the staff on its toes, be prepared for a challenge every hour and an opportunity every day. Be prepared for the unexpected, the situation you have never encountered before.

This volume deals with general personnel administrators who set policy and organize personnel practices, and also with supervisors providing immediate direction

1

along the line, the general officer responsible for staff, and the department head in cataloging, in reference and other divisions. The two are partners; they are interconnected and face the same problems. In smaller libraries the personnel administrator and the supervisor may be one and the same person.

The great variety of humankind among staff members is matched by the great variety among personnel administrators and supervisors. The text will seek to identify and develop the traits needed by all who deal with staff, and actually presents a quiz for these officers in Chapter 8, but few paragons come along who meet all the desirable requirements. There are supervisors who get work done even though they are curt and aloof, and others who lead staff to goals even though they don't have the gift of clear and easy communication. There are exceptions among personnel administrators to any of the listed traits, yet they prevail because they have an extra measure of various other attributes. Don't try to fit a neat pattern. In any list of desirable traits of supervisors, you will lack some. Play from your strength.

But this does not mean that personnel administrators should arbitrarily brush aside certain desirable traits because they do not readily fit their own personalities. On the contrary, it is precisely those attributes in which the individual is weakest that should be studied and nurtured. The more a golfer or a runner or a singer knows about the skills involved in his or her activity, the better he or she will perform and develop a personal style that is effective. The same goes for personnel administration, which at times can seem like a combination of a sport and an art.

Most readers of this book will have dealt with at least a few people at some time, perhaps way back in a school activity or in a neighborhood project, and now in a library group. Each such experience has probably added some insight on how to get work done through others, and perhaps also some frustrations arising from the vagaries of human response.

An effort is made here to pull together the growing

understanding of what makes people function in the workplace. This comes not solely from the perception of one person, the author, although his experience in the administration of libraries and of library schools, and then a decade in publishing, has built a certain insight, as have some years of consultation with libraries in trouble. More of the understanding is derived from the voluminous literature of personnel administration. Particularly since mid-century, in the period after World War II, not only management theorists (Drucker, Barnard, Yoder) but also psychologists (Maslow, Likert, McGregor) have focused on personnel as the heart of enterprise. There is a wealth of wisdom to digest and bring together in a coherent discipline. Or perhaps into an art, which is even harder to make coherent.

It is interesting that the amount of publication on personnel administration has decreased in the 1980s and the 1990s. Is this because all there was to learn has become known? Or is it because the 1980s saw an unnatural excess of business and industrial and institutional growth, followed by a prolonged economic recession and a decline of support for institutions, including libraries, that suggests that not enough is known about people on the job?

In either case libraries will go on, in some form. They need to be staffed, they need to respond to developments of the next years. Personnel administration must not only continue, it will be subject to severe tests in the period ahead. We need to pull together what we know about human relations and job performance in the interest of the institutions to which we are dedicated.

AIMS AND OBJECTIVES

Even before people must come goals and objectives. What is the library for—what is it trying to do—where is it going next—which programs should get priority and which should be downgraded?

Answers to such questions affect personnel administra-

tion all along the line. Depending on purpose and program, the kinds of staff members selected will differ, as
will training programs within the library, and performance standards, and policies for promotion, and even
salaries paid.

Very few agencies have thought through such considerations. The library is there, the doors are open, users come
in, the agency seeks to serve them. The institution is
well-established and the service program has not changed
much over the years. The assumption is that it will go on
about the same in the future. Why then bother to review
aims and objectives?

As a result, few libraries have explicit statements of
objectives. When pressed, their officials would respond
that they are there to provide service, to serve their
clientele. For any kind of demand? What if a portion of the
public seeks pornography and sexually-explicit illustra-
tions? What if the college student seeks help in establishing a drug ring on campus?

Such questions are likely to be dismissed as far-fetched.
But how far will the library go with the services it does
provide? Will very obscure material be found for the
researcher? What degree of help will be given to students
doing term papers? Should children be taught to improve
their reading skills by the librarian? These and similar
questions come back to decisions about purpose.

Public Library Objectives

The point can be best illustrated with the case of the
public library, which has the most diffuse and undefined
purposes. Other agencies, such as school and academic
and special libraries, are likely to take their objectives
from their parent institutions, riding piggy-back on institutional mission and goals. Yet even here objectives and
priorities are often vague and undefined, and come under
scrutiny only when budgets are reduced.

Confronted with the question of just what business they
are in, public libraries fall back on generalities. They are
there to provide service, they say. To answer the needs of

their communities. On further reflection, a variety of contrasting purposes are likely to be claimed:

1. to serve constituents following subject interests
2. to furnish information as requested
3. to provide wholesome recreational material
4. to nurture reading on the part of children
5. to provide guidance in educational pursuits
6. to back up the school library with advanced materials needed for projects and term papers
7. to guide and counsel searchers in the use of proliferating data bases
8. to serve as a community center for cultural and intellectual interests

The immediate reaction to such a list is that it is very ambitious and goes in many directions. As a list of purposes, is it feasible, achievable? When aims are very diffuse, achieving them is that much harder.

One looks over the list to see if any of these objectives can legitimately be passed over to other agencies. This might be applied to the goal of serving as a supplement to school resources, on the ground that the school should meet its own needs (on the contrary, some schools have reduced their own library provision because the community agency is there). Similar possibilities might be considered in such functions as serving as community center or taking responsibility for nurturing reading in children (actually such nurturing occurs in the home and the school, and the public library gets those youngsters who have responded to the nurturing). Or the hard-headed analyst might point to possible reduction in provision of recreational material, which is available in every supermarket and drug store.

Another reaction to such a list is that the sharp differences in mission suggested would logically lead to contrasting service programs and would even affect the physical facilities provided. If recreational reading is the objective, a large central collection would not be called for, nor even large branches; small collections might be deposited in stores, churches, offices and other local outlets, as indeed was done at one time in the past. Or a very different function, that of guiding and counseling in the use of computerized data sources, which will be coming more and more into all of our lives, would not call for a library as we have known the agency, but rather for consultation offices such as those providing other professional services (lawyers', doctors', dentists' offices).

It is instructive to run through such a list of objectives as that above and think of the differing kinds of staff members and the differing kinds of personnel programs that would apply. If the emphasis is on passive provision of material requested, you need traditional librarians— knowledgeable about sources for locating publications, and themselves casual readers in a wide range of subjects—but if the emphasis is to be on educational stimulation and guidance, you need librarians trained in the psychology of learning and engaged in more systematic pursuit of interests similar to the kind of study practiced by their strongly-motivated clients. These are two quite different qualities to seek out in staff members. Or again, if the library is to be a source of information from the usual collection of reference and subject books, you need librarians skilled in reference methods, familiar with the sources on the shelves, and quick to understand client requests; whereas if the library looks to the future when its dependence will be more and more on computerized data sources, staff members must not only be conversant with the many automated files accessible from outside the library but must also be skilled in search techniques. Again the emphasis is quite different.

The kind of staff sought, the level of training needed, the job titles, will depend on what the library is trying to do.

The influential management consultant, Peter Drucker, stresses the importance of first clarifying goals and objectives, particularly in service institutions. He urges administrators to ask, "What is our business and what should it be?" He even has a section on "Organized Abandonment," by which he means having a plan to decide what past activities can now be minimized or eliminated.[1] Library directors had better have some "organized abandonment" sessions directed at just what they will seek and will not seek to do. Goals and objectives can guide retrenchment as well as growth. This is not the place to prescribe what the goals of public libraries or any libraries should be. The procedure for reaching conclusions on these basic considerations were covered in still another volume in this series: *Library Planning and Policy Making*, by Kathleen Molz, 1990. The essential point is for each community and library board and staff to decide on its own aims.

Objectives in all Libraries

Unless clearly articulated aims and priorities exist, personnel decisions must be made in a kind of twilight zone, hoping that this new employee selected, this staff member designated for promotion, this standard for evaluating performance will really contribute to what the library is trying to do. In fact, the uncertainty applies not just to the present but also to what the library program will be ten or twenty years hence, well within the working life of the individual just being added to the payroll.

It is not enough for a library to have only a general plan of development, say to meet more of the needs of the constituency in the years ahead. Be skeptical of a goal that is simply "more" of the same, both because it is too vague to challenge staff, and because a change in emphasis rather than more of the same may be called for by changes in the constituency, in the kind and form of resources on the market, and by downright restrictions in the budget.

What is needed is a clear statement of aims, objectives and priorities. This applies to school, academic and special libraries as well as to the community agency.

There is another and more mundane reason for looking to aims and objectives. Financial support for libraries has been difficult to get in recent years, and will continue so unless the U.S. economy expands substantially. Libraries are having to do with smaller increases than in the past, and in some cases actually with reduced funds. The response up to this time has been contraction. Hours of

service are reduced, book budgets and periodical subscription lists are cut, expensive data bases are dropped,
some positions have been eliminated. If this continues for
extended period, libraries will be shells of their former
selves.

All the more reason, then, to re-examine goals and
objectives and to go on to priorities. Increasingly, administrators must have a fundamental sequence built into
their bones. The sequence is simply this:

1. Establish goals, long-term aims
2. Set up objectives to achieve the goals; the more concrete
   and measurable the better
3. Press through to priorities; what must be done first and
   done when funds are short
4. Design programs that will contribute to the objectives
5. After a reasonable period, apply measures to find out
   whether the plan is working

RECURRING THEMES

Certain themes will occur and recur throughout this book.
It is worthwhile to introduce them at this early stage,
thereby helping the reader to recognize them as they come
up in the context of different settings and different techniques, and helping also to show how they can be
achieved in different ways.

Human Relations

Over the years an understanding has grown up of what
motivates staff members in the workplace. While material
rewards are important, it is clear that most workers seek
more than the regular paycheck. In that we all spend a
considerable part of our time on the job, we naturally seek
some satisfactions and accomplishments in employment.
In fact, some people gain more fulfillment in their careers
than in their personal and social lives.

On the other hand, where personal satisfactions are

lacking, workers lose motivation and fall into routine performance, doing no more than necessary to avoid disciplinary action, never going the extra step that makes for maximum service. They require extra supervision to attain full productivity. They are quick to complain or protest if conditions are not to their liking and, once in the routine, they tend to resist change that disrupts the comfortable work pattern that they have developed. This condition can appear in professionals (who then like to call it "burn-out") as well as in support staff.

The personnel administrator should sit back at intervals and ask how many of his/her subordinates fall into this group. Here is where extra effort is needed. Not everyone can be encouraged or jolted out of marginal performance, but the supervisor is not justified in criticizing or taking more drastic action until the extra effort is made. The sub-par performer may be a reflection of sub-par personnel administration.

The theory of human relations has been developed step-by-step over the past century. Psychologists have provided a basis and practical administrators have added applications. The results apply in libraries as surely as in offices, schools and factories.

This development is traced in the third chapter of this book, and references are provided that deserve further attention. To a degree every personnel administrator should be a human-relations expert.

Self-Motivated Staff

The application of human relations, it is hoped, produces a self-motivated staff. This is another theme that will occur and recur throughout the volume.

Theoretically, if every staff member were strongly motivated, an enterprise could dispense with supervision. Everyone would give full effort, everyone would cooperate with others, everyone would evaluate what is achieved and make adjustments for improvement. This is what happens when the football team performs at full capacity.

But neither Red Grange in the past nor Joe Montana today can keep the team at maximum effectiveness. Even the champions lose games.

Self-motivation is a factor that turns up at every phase of personnel administration. At the starting point of recruitment and selection, the administrator should seek individuals with built-in discipline. Not just the paper record, not just the pleasant personality, but look also for evidence that individuals have a capacity that prompts them to complete jobs once started, a natural standard of carrying through. In orientation and instruction, stress should be placed on the responsibility of individuals to go it on their own. The same quality should be included in periodic evaluations of performance.

The inner standard applies all through the staff, from the neophyte to the specialist. The person shelving books, without being watched over, should look around to locate all material not in its place; equally, the librarian working with a researcher should reach out to the elusive and obscure.

Staff members who display self-motivation require less supervision. More than that, they are happier on the job because no one is standing over them, checking their performance. You want staff members who get satisfaction from exercising their own volition and resolution.

On the other hand, you do not want subordinates who need to be pushed and then checked and re-directed. In fact, you can hardly implant and build up self-motivation if it is not there. Get it in the beginning, nurture it, and reward it.

Workers, professional and others, come to the library with a certain sympathy with its goals and programs—or they would be in another vocation. They certainly do not come because library salaries are so high. The task of personnel administration is to bring this natural sympathy together with the aims and programs of the individual library, to close the gap between the hopes and expectations that workers bring and the job itself. The more this can be achieved, the more staff members will be motivated. This is an underlying theme in the chapters that follow.

Supervisor as Facilitator

One view of personnel administration is that it is the process of opening the path along which staff members can move forward. This concept of facilitator—rather than boss or overseer or controller—will animate much of what follows. This interpretation of supervisor is almost a contradiction of the role usually ascribed to the person in charge.

This concept is introduced here at the beginning because, like self-motivation, it is one of the essential ingredients of modern personnel administration. And it is related to the aim of a self-motivated staff in that workers who have some momentum of their own welcome a clear path for improvement and respond to help from their supervisor. In fact, the two interact on each other: the facilitator nurtures self-motivation, and the motivated persons increase their mobility with this help.

The supervisor presents the goals and standards of the library at the outset. These qualities are inculcated and deepened in the training period when staff members are instructed in their duties. The career ladder opened up before recruits has the same effect—that is, opening the way forward. Another opportunity comes when counseling an individual who may not be coming up to standard. The annual evaluation session is in effect a joint planning of next steps in service.

This emphasis on facilitation does not mean that the personnel administrator becomes a bystander or cheerleader. The supervisor embodies the objectives of the agency, and has the responsibility to hold workers to these goals. Facilitation combines some attributes of leadership and of pushing. If particular workers do not respond, the person in charge must see to it that re-assignment, or even displacement, occurs. There does come a moment when authority enters the relationship.

Participatory Management

Do not picture the supervisor-subordinate relationship as one individual at the top and others below, following orders. Picture it rather as the personnel manager or supervisor in the middle with workers round about in a kind of circle, with lines of communication in two directions, back and forth between personnel administrator and staff members.

There are various points where staff members have a contribution to make to planning and to decisions. In dealing with a problem that has arisen or in preparing for a new activity, workers who have been on the service line may have a first-hand grasp of what will work. When interviewing recruits for appointment the reaction of selected staff members can add to insight. The same benefit can accrue in bringing staff into decisions on promotion, the way academic faculty members participate in decisions on who will receive tenure. Even in discussions on objectives or in making those hard decisions on what to curtail when budgets are cut, the views of workers deserve consideration. There is a wealth of human resources in those who work at the service desks, in touch day after day with users, that should be utilized.

A whole array of techniques can be brought into play to achieve this purpose: staff meetings, visits to other libraries, committees, suggestion boxes, conferences with representatives of the public. A guiding statement about purpose and program may well be the result, with staff well informed about its content, and with staff morale enhanced because members feel that they have made a contribution.

The author recalls one example of participation that impressed him. In a large branch public library, I noted that the bi-weekly staff meetings often brought out incidental observations and suggestions from members about needs and problems in the agency. The suggestion was made by the group that these be jotted down when they occurred to the worker and simply deposited in a convenient box. The idea was adopted enthusiastically by the group and the box was heavily used, producing leads that were taken up at subsequent staff meetings.

This useful device so impressed me that I proposed it at another branch for which I was responsible. The suggestion was accepted by the group, but with little enthusiasm. It turned out that the box was very little used. Why not? Hardly because the agency was so perfect that there was little room for improvement. I believe that the difference was that in one case the idea came from the staff as a whole, while in the other it was imposed by administration.

Turning to staff to participate in planning assumes that workers seek a purpose, a mission in their job. While this may not be true for every staff member on the library payroll, it does hold for many and, one hopes, for most of the professionals. Such individuals seek a sense of satisfaction in their working lives, a sense of contributing to a worthy purpose, and they are likely to be particularly dedicated to goals they themselves have help set.

There is a further dividend. Staff members who have contributed to the defining of goals and objectives, and who personally subscribe to the resulting document, will need less control and supervision. With aims clearly defined, and participants devoted to them, work will get done, and workers may even seek to coordinate their efforts with those of other employees. This brings us closer to the self-motivated staff.

Why do workers at the charge desk work steadily and as rapidly as circumstances permit? Because the work intrigues them? Not likely. Because they fear dismissal if they goof off? Perhaps, but few agencies jump to such extreme action. No, the motivation of the workers is a combination of their own personal standards for performance with the belief that their work adds to the purposes of the library.

Sound personnel administration naturally seeks to select workers with high personal standards. This takes care of one side of the equation. Then the other side must be added. The task of supervision is to show that the work is important to the library, and thus to the individual. Personal and institutional goals come together. If the individual accepts this, conditions are right for productivity. The worker has in a sense adopted the goal of the library. The combination of individual and enterprise is made.

This does not mean that every idea coming from the ranks should be put into effect. But each responsible suggestion should be given consideration. If ideas from staff are not adopted, the reasons should be made clear. Participatory management does not mean dictation from below, but it does involve serious consultation. Drawing out the staff is a delicate task for personnel administrators, for it involves a balance of open-mindedness combined with retention of authority.

From the standpoint of staff members, the results are usually favorable. They feel that it is a vote of confidence that they are consulted, and they put an extra measure of effort into projects to which they have contributed. Even the individual whose suggestion has not been adopted is likely to go along if the decision was reached in open discussion.

This joining of goals of the individual and of the enterprise is made easier if staff members participate in setting or reviewing institutional aims and policies. Should the library stress more the needs of serious students who need to borrow books for longer periods? Desk assistants can contribute to discussion of extending the loan period both because they have relevant observations based on their experiences at the loan desk and because they are the ones who will carry out any new policy. Should reference staff take responsibility for showing patrons how to use resources as well as pointing out what is available? Once again staff members closest to user transactions will be in a position to judge the commitment of time that is involved.

Mobilize the full resources of staff. Both the institution and the individual will get a boost.

Empathy

All of this will be possible if personnel administrators can reach out and see matters from the standpoint of the individuals being dealt with. Empathy will carry supervisors over rough spots and smooth the path into any new activity.

This ability does not come naturally. We all are self-centered to a degree; we look out at the world and at other people from our own perspective. Now we are being asked to look through the eyes of the other person.

Surprisingly, the other person may be right. Or, if not right, the other view may throw light on the matter in hand. Desk assistants may genuinely feel that the policy of referring all service questions to the reference desk, even if they know the answer, diminishes their role. This is the occasion for reviewing respective responsibilities and contributions. The children's librarian may feel constrained in restricting even exceptional young readers to juvenile books. Looking at this through the eyes of the staff member may lead to rules for making exceptions to the general policy, or it may even lead to changing the policy itself. Be sure to turn on the empathy when criticizing a subordinate, not in order to excuse whatever is being criticized, but perhaps to modify the way the reprimand is presented, depending on the sensitivity of the individual. Part of the success of personnel administration depends on recognizing the variety of humankind.

Other necessary qualities of the supervisor may be contrary to concern for the outlook and feelings of others. The supervisor needs a considerable measure of self-confidence and the ability to make decisions and push projects through to completion. This should be tempered by an equal measure of empathy. This is a kind of maturity that the personnel administrator should nurture. Indeed, maturity in both judgment and emotions will be implied throughout the following pages.

The text will shortly get to principles and techniques that require these qualities, but first a chapter will be devoted to the emergence of the librarian as professional, followed by a chapter reviewing the human relations movement that has animated personnel administration in recent decades.

Throughout, a measure of realism will be injected. Empathy does not extend to excusing shoddy work; the library is not a place for workers who goof off. The aim is to pull together, and those who will not should not be tolerated—in fact, one hopes they will be caught in the selection process and not admitted to the staff. Building the team is half the game.

REFERENCES

1. Peter F. Drucker, *Management; Tasks, Responsibilities, Practices* (New York: Harper and Row, 1974), 158–166.

2. EMERGENCE OF THE LIBRARIAN

Libraries have existed, if not from the beginning of time, at least since the beginning of records, no matter what their form. Whether tablets or papyrus, the records were preserved for purposes of government, commerce and religion. A collection was established, and it was consulted from time to time.

The earliest libraries were no more than places of storage, archives at best. Someone had to designate the location of the collections and gather the records, and logically can be expected, at least in some cases, to have given some kind of order to them.

The responsible individual was not called a "librarian" until much later. The more common term was library-keeper, and the title was appropriate because the job was to keep the material. The title of Demetrius, who built up the great Alexandrian Library, was "Keeper of the Books."[1]

Anyone might be designated the Keeper, from a servant to a scholar, from a monk to a government official. In church libraries the choirmaster was often also called on to add the care of books to his collection of musical scores. Some of the earliest collections did not have much need of Keepers, for the manuscripts were kept chained to tables and desks and could not readily be removed. If one wanted to read a manuscript, it was common to send a servant to copy it laboriously by hand.

CHANGES OVER THE YEARS

Monks predominated as keepers of the monastic libraries of the Middle Ages. As noted by the eminent medieval historian:

Only in later times do we find the librarian distinguished from the cantor and the library from the scriptorium, and then only in the greater monasteries. The impulse given by the Carolingian renaissance toward wider learning gave monastic libraries new dignity and importance, and accordingly, the armarius began to appear as a separate official and the library techniques were gradually developed.[2]

Then, as universities appeared at the beginning of the Renaissance—the University of Paris, Oxford, Cambridge—scholars came to the fore as chief librarians. The same applied in the first universities in America, established before the Revolution—Harvard (1638), Yale (1701), Princeton (1746). At Harvard the first director designated as Librarian was appointed in 1667.

Along the way elements of library practice slowly came into place and these accumulated into the beginnings of a recognized library economy. Again quoting from James Westfall Thompson:

The development of the catalogue from the crude shelf list to a true subject-and-author catalogue did not take place generally until after the invention of printing, though in a few instances there were earlier anticipations of the new method.[3]

The philosopher Gottfried Leibniz, who took charge of the Duke of Hanover's library at Wolfenbuttel in 1679, is credited with introducing the concept of the organized reference library.[4]

A few great private collections appeared in the 18th and 19th centuries and in time evolved into organized libraries—the Astor and Lenox Foundation in New York, the Newberry Library in Chicago and the Huntington on the West Coast. Historians were favored as the directors of these institutions.

On the public library side, the agency in Peterborough, New Hampshire, established in 1833, is usually recognized as the original because it was the pioneer library open to the public and supported by tax funds (actually the state bank tax).[5] Forerunners had appeared previously, without primary support from tax funds, in the form of church and social libraries, proprietary subscription and mechanics' collections, back to Benjamin Franklin's Library Company (1731). The keepers of these collections were a mixed crew, and no doubt some earned the appellation of "librarian."

School libraries appeared at about the time of the first public libraries, following Horace Mann's call in Massachusetts in 1839. Over the years they have developed into the modern concept of school media centers. For the earlier period teachers maintained the embryonic collections.

But the appearance of librarians as professionals—that is, as a distinct group, with defined educational requirements and possessing mastery of a body of theory and methodology—is hardly more than a century old. At the 1883 conference of the American Library Association, Melvil Dewey triumphantly proclaimed, "... the time has come when a librarian may, without assumption, speak of his occupation as a professional," but he may have been premature. Even today the term "librarian" still means to many people the keeper of the book, the manager of a place called a library, in the same way that there are grocers and druggists and bankers managing their domains. The only difference in the popular view is that the librarian is typically pictured as a woman, while the other proprietors are seen as men—one more evidence of sexism.

But recognition of librarianship as a profession is now present in some quarters. State laws have endowed librarians with certification requirements, and civil service classifications in city and state jurisdictions specify such a group, along with the special education needed for membership. Moreover, various credentials of a profession have appeared, in the Master's degree, in a national association, in a body of literature devoted to the field. And there is self-recognition by librarians, who consider themselves part of a distinctive group and know who they accept into the fold and who they do not.

The continued emergence of the librarian can be traced in the growth of education for the profession.

EDUCATION FOR LIBRARIANS

A kind of false start was made in formal training for librarians at Columbia University in 1887. This program shifted to the New York State Library after two brief years when Melvil Dewey transferred there. His training program at Columbia lost support in part because it included female students and in part because the place of vocational training was not clear in an academic structure that stressed research. The school in Albany provided apprentice training in conjunction with an on-going library. For several decades this center produced individuals who called themselves librarians and who were recognized in some quarters as such. In the early years of the century, other academic programs for librarians appeared, at Simmons College in 1902 and Emory University in 1905. The growth was slow until the 1920s with librarianship gradually gaining status as a learned profession.

Early on, training classes appeared in several city libraries. They were designed to provide background and applied skills to many new employees with only high-school or partial college education. Actually the training classes made a contribution. For example, promising young women were given instruction in children's literature and in activities for young readers, and the libraries thereby had personnel to handle the children's service programs that proliferated in the 1920s. Others were given training in reference service and management practices and shortly ended up at reference desks or in charge of the branch libraries proliferating in cities. Some of the municipal training classes took in students from other nearby agencies, including some academic libraries. Thus a corps of trained practitioners appeared in the library world, in a period when libraries were gaining a foothold and support. The trainees carried the institution through the depression years, when use of the public agencies gained several-fold.

In 1923, a fresh start was made at Columbia University, with Melvil Dewey off the scene, and with a grant from the Carnegie Corporation. The University by this time had moved into the 20th century and tolerated women students. The Williamson Report[6] convincingly made the case for graduate study as a requisite for professional library service.

In the next years, the movement for advanced academic study rolled forward. By 1952 there were 31 university programs accredited by the American Library Association, and the number almost doubled in the coming years. Some, like that at Columbia, called for a year of graduate study, a few called for two years, and some (Type III schools) incorporated the training into the undergraduate years. A new generation of librarians appeared on the scene.

Education for librarianship was given a further boost with a shift in the 1960s to the Master's degree. Formerly the credential for a year of graduate study was a second Bachelor's degree. Actually, little change was made in the library curriculum, nor were faculties notably strengthened, but graduates now had the label of a higher professional degree.

In those same years, the American Library Association was growing in size and impact. The new library-school graduates had a professional association to which they could give their allegiance, and which in turn reinforced their sense of belonging to a distinct calling. National leaders came to the fore. Various journals appeared. Librarianship was taking hold.

To crown the development, the Graduate Library School at the University of Chicago came onto the scene in the 1930s. It also had a grant behind it, and shortly had a statesman dean in Louis R. Wilson. The purpose was not basic professional training, but advanced and research work leading to the doctorate. The faculty in part was recruited from basic disciplines: sociology (Douglas

Waples), political science (Carleton Joeckel), and history (Pierce Butler). Within two decades a body of theory and principle for librarianship emerged from the school and began to provide the academic underpinning that the profession lacked. Then the Graduate Library School was tempted into basic professional education, thus diffusing its resources, and after a period was seduced by a new development called information science. Having stretched itself too thin, the school lost its distinctive vitality. In particular, it failed to produce significant research, which would have increased its stature in an institution as research-oriented as the University of Chicago. The University discontinued the school, starting the trend toward library-school closings.

In the last decade, education for librarianship has in a sense come full circle. A half-dozen well-established graduate programs have been discontinued, including the original school at Columbia University. Several factors account for this reversal, including financial pressures on higher education, lack of eminence and research productivity on the part of library-school faculties, and the isolation of the schools within the universities. The basic cause is the slight body of theory and principle behind library instruction; the universities simply do not see an intellectual content in librarianship. Over a century of graduate work has not produced an ideational foundation for the profession.

QUESTIONS ABOUT PROFESSIONAL STATUS

So library keepers have over the years emerged into a profession. Librarians consider themselves as members of a defined and recognized group. Whether the general public thinks of librarians as professionals is another question. A hard-headed look at the librarian who has emerged may throw light on questions of status and recognition, and will also provide background for personnel administration within libraries.

In the public eye, the agency of the library generally has

a favorable image, which may or may not extend to staff members. The library itself is looked on with respect, as a place with useful resources and as an asset in the community, the school and the university. Users enter libraries with a sense of appreciation and expectation.

As to the image or prestige of librarians themselves, an ambivalent situation must be reported. Many people have an automatic but lukewarm respect for librarians, holding them to be worthy workers, but in reality workers without major responsibility and without need for extensive education. No serious results, positive or negative, follow their ministrations. They are seen as useful but not critical members of society.

There is even a strain of holding the librarian up to a form of ridicule, as mousy and dowdy, prim and proper. A recent television advertisement for the hairdressing of a major cosmetics company has a frowsy-headed model say, "I look like a librarian." In Neil Simon's play *Plaza Suite,* when the daughter's marriage is in the balance, the fathers says with desperation, "She will probably become a librarian." This form of image is projected even though the next librarian the advertiser or playwright meets may be chic, self-assured, even aggressive. Evidently society needs scapegoats just as it needs heroes.

Most librarians don't worry too much about image, although they may well grouse about salary. They get back to work and see if they can analyze the next new book thoroughly or handle the next tough reference question.

Within the library field itself a different question arose. Earlier studies of duties actually performed by librarians showed that professionals often engaged in various activities for which the MLS degree was clearly not essential. This does not solely refer to such clearly clerical duties as filing, typing and physical arrangement of materials, although such were actually mixed into the more complex responsibilities. Even more challenging today is whether routine reference work, drawing on a shelf-full of common reference sources, or simple entry into the computer of title-page information to produce the automated record, are "professional."

In the past such questions were not raised. Then, as demands on libraries increased, and particularly when financial support became more difficult to get, the matter of who and what is professional was looked at more closely. As a result the proportion of professional positions in medium-sized and larger libraries has steadily decreased in recent decades, from an earlier proportion of 50 per cent or more down to one-quarter of total staff. On the face of it, this is evidence that the earlier proportion was neither justified nor efficient. Non-professional duties have been to a degree cut out of professional jobs and assigned to lower-paid workers without advanced degrees.

The adjustment is still going on. To this day, distinction of duties by level is not too clear. Physicians are assisted and in a sense protected by several categories of lesser-trained staff, such as nurses, laboratory technicians, and physician assistants. No such formal structure of support personnel has emerged for librarians, so that technical tasks not requiring graduate study still appear among their duties.

Among the non-librarian or support staff prevalent in libraries, categories and levels are often unclear and not standardized. Some libraries simply have a clerical or non-professional group, with members over a considerable range, from typists to desk attendants to specialized technicians. In some agencies an intermediate level has been established, requiring qualifications beyond basic clerical skills but short of library-school education. For a period "library assistant" training was offered in two-year community colleges, but this has not expanded because suitable positions have not been widely established.

But librarians have the Master's degree to hold up as evidence of professional status. Or do they? Outside voices—of subject specialists, of government personnel agencies—have on occasion challenged the academic symbol. What about a subject master's degree in positions closely related to the subject content of resources? Is a person with advanced academic work in a science collection in a university and serving science faculty and students to be excluded from the professional library ranks? In a general reference or cataloging position in a public library, what about the college graduate with a liberal-arts degree plus some experience under supervision on the job? The line is fuzzy and ill-defined.

What these various questions come back to is the underlying lack of a body of library theory and principles. What is it that distinguishes the librarian?—what intellectual competence, what specialized knowledge? Is it a sufficient response to point to familiarity with classification schemes and some degree of knowledge of sources of information? Is there a skill involved that can be reduced to a body of principles?

NATURE OF PROFESSIONAL SERVICE

Stand back and analyze the situation in a typical library service encounter, say a man coming to the reference desk of a medium-sized public library, or a young woman at the service desk of the college library. He wants guidance in materials about space flight, or impressionistic art, or the finishing of a basement in this home; she needs material on some aspect of psychology or astronomy related to her course work.

What does the reference librarian know about any of these topics? Probably very little about space flight or finishing basements or psychology. The librarian can point to the catalog or the requisite shelf space or a relevant index. Let's say the material is new to the inquirers, so they ask what would be a good starting point. Librarians have little with which to work at this point; they know nothing about the individual whom they may now be seeing for the first time. And the librarian has had little training in the learning process by which the materials can be used effectively.

Contrast this with the patient being attended by a doctor. The physician has studied the disease before him or her (or, if not, refers the patient to a specialist). The physician knows the individual from previous visits or has just obtained a detailed physical history. The patient will be asked to come back so that the doctor knows whether the prescribed remedy worked—and the doctor adds this to memory in treating future patients with similar symptoms. Or take the case of a high-school student going for help to a teacher. The latter probably has some background in the subject at issue, at least at the school level, knows the student from classroom performance, and has been trained in the learning process. Subject matter, individual inquirer, the probable effect of the sources recommended—all known to the professional. But not if that professional is a general reference librarian in the usual library setting, seeing the inquirer for the first time, and perhaps never again.

This is not to imply that the other professionals are always omniscient and invariably work out the right solution. But they do have the knowledge and background needed. Nor is this to imply that the librarian cannot always help. However, the two situations are not the same; the librarian is at a distinct disadvantage, without discipline in the subject being explored and without knowledge of the inquirer. In the eye of the patron, the librarian is more like a traffic policeman directing people to appropriate locations.

In library education, some effort is made to transmit a body of theory. But this comes not so much from librarianship but from related fields such as communication, education, linguistics, management, psychology, sociology and other disciplines. This reaching out to other fields is all to the good but it does not result in a discipline distinct to librarianship. This is what lies behind the challenges to librarianship as a profession and to the closing of library schools by several major universities.

CAREERS OF LIBRARIANS

It will be noted in the next chapter that the human relations movement in personnel administration has led to emphasis on challenging careers. What is the prospect for able and ambitious young people entering the library profession?

Many thousands of recruits have found satisfaction as professional librarians. Surveys among practitioners show that the vast majority have no regrets about their choice. Very few callings have a higher satisfaction vote.

Librarians find the work rewarding, they had a wide choice in the kind of service they entered, and also considerable choice as to geographic location. Or at least they had such choice until the supply of trained recruits recently came to exceed the number of openings. They find themselves a part of a national association which now has over 55,000 members, and often of state or local groups in addition. A bond holds most librarians together, a feeling of being part of a recognized vocation. Much of this can be traced to the fact that most librarians make a conscious choice to enter what they conceive to be a service enterprise, and it turns out in actual practice that this proves to be the case. The day-to-day work provides satisfaction.

Particularly for women the field has offered opportunity. In earlier years not many professions were open to women; this is one in which they are a majority. Some have welcomed the chance to leave for a period to raise a family and then to return to the ranks. Besides the gratification of the daily work, some women have moved to the top of the career ladder as directors of large university and municipal and state libraries. The elected presidents of the American Library Association in the past ten years have included six women.

When the spotlight is shifted to salary, a less sanguine situation exists. Starting salaries after a year of graduate study have been consistently below those for most other professions.

Even after ten or 15 years, compensation in the profession in many cases is less than $40,000 a year at the present time. Librarians who take on major administrative responsibilities, perhaps handling annual budgets of several million dollars, still do not make as much as middle managers in business and industry, and markedly less than well-established practitioners in medicine and law. Librarianship cannot be held up to young people as a lucrative calling; the appeal must rest on the work performed, the psychic returns of rendering service, and working with people seeking knowledge.

Library staff members, like employees in most enterprises, look forward to a career—that is, to a continuing work relationship with opportunities for advancement. But the fact remains that the career ladder in librarianship has very few rungs, short of major administrative responsibilities. After a decade or so of service, most professionals reach a plateau, encounter a kind of ceiling.

An analysis of the usual structure of library positions confirms the problem. Professionals have the prospect of two levels of employment—termed Junior Librarian and Senior Librarian or sometimes Librarian I and II—and then they must take on definite administrative duties if they want to go further. Here is where they hit the ceiling, sometimes after only a half-dozen years of practice. This applies equally to those who seek administrative responsibility, and therefore welcome the situation, and to those attracted to the profession precisely because it is a service rather than an administrative field. Some individuals resist shifting to the management ranks because they know that the library director and the department head may go for months or more without once appraising a new publication or engaging in bibliographic or service work. Others are tempted to shift to administration because of salary and prestige, even though they may not have aptitude in that direction. One wonders how many fine librarians there are who are performing as mediocre administrators.

Those who resist the move settle into positions that have no future, and they see little point in seeking to make an extra contribution. Many libraries have a cadre of professionals of middle years or beyond who do their job, but no more. If the agency sees them as routine troops, they will serve in this capacity. It is as though a lawyer cannot get ahead unless appointed as vice-president of the firm, or a doctor cannot get ahead unless appointed administrator of the hospital.

This problem will be analyzed in more depth in Chapter 4, on Organization of Positions, and a solution to the problem is proposed there.

TYPES OF LIBRARY WORK

Which kind or type of library employment is most desirable, most satisfying? The academic position, with its association with subject materials and research? The public library post, with its wide variety of human contacts? The school library, where one can build a small empire of one's own? The special library, with its concentration of service on the goals of a business or technical or scholarly enterprise? Of course, there is no answer. It depends on the fit between the individual librarian and the individual job.

One of the attractions of librarianship is the wide variety of settings and opportunities that exist. Think of the differences in experiences and satisfactions of a librarian on a bookmobile in a rural county and a reference assistant in the Library of Congress, of the differences between the headship of a small college library and a cataloger in a large city collection. The spectrum is wide and many-hued. There is a place for the person who wants a corner where he or she can do a thorough, intense job and for an individual who wants to reach out to new worlds, for the introvert and the extrovert, for the traditionalist and the explorer. One can even leave the field for a period (to raise a family, to try a business venture) and return to the ranks. That is, these many opportunities are available if the economy remains sound and if libraries have reasonable financial support.

In view of this variety, it is interesting that not many librarians shift from one kind of library to another or from one specialty to another. There is the progression from professional service to administrative work, but usually this occurs in the same library or the same type of library. The roads between different kinds of service become more separate as the years go by, so that a shift from type to type becomes less likely. Librarians in their thirties are on the track that they will follow for the rest of their careers. One can only hope that the choice they have made will bring them to their personal goals.

Full advantage is not taken by librarians of the rich variety of jobs in the field. The lesson here for personnel administrators is to keep the barriers down between classes of positions and between types of libraries; the best person for a senior reference position may be over in the bibliographic unit, the best person for a public-library directorship may be a department head in the nearby university library. Most people probably prefer to remain in the type of library and the kind of position they have selected, but some may wish they could change tracks.

Testimony on the advantages and rewards of each kind of library work would best come from individuals within each type. The academic librarian might stress the daily immersion in subject resources, selecting and guiding in topics with which the individual is familiar. The public librarian might stress the public, with the widest of interests and idiosyncrasies. The special librarian would comment on the satisfaction of providing the specific material needed by a member of the organization.

Some recruits to the profession, remembering with nostalgia their period as library helpers in high school, may consciously aim at a school position. This puts them in the middle of an educational institution, and education is their dominant interest. The school position offers a unit of one's own, a piece of territory for which, within limits, one can set goals and design and conduct programs. There is the satisfaction of running one's own shop. At the same time, the position still keeps the librarian in essential library tasks: building the collection, organizing resources for use, providing materials for special projects, handling complex reference inquiries. Associations are compatible, with teachers and students at their best. This holds true if some clerical help is provided, which is not always the case.

If the typical school librarian were offered a position as head of a medium-sized public library in town, or as head of a department in the local university, he or she might well hesitate. Such assignments, being primarily administrative, would probably not include regular participation in essential library services. And, assuming the individual were well-enough established to be offered such opportunities, there would probably be very little advance in salary.

Running through the responses, from whatever part of the spectrum, would be the emphasis on service. The satisfaction of the librarian is in meeting human needs. The staff member goes home at night in the security of having been useful, and for the kinds of individuals attracted to librarianship this may be satisfying even though their neighbors may be getting larger salary checks. Working conditions are acceptable, hours are within reason, pressures are not too great. For the right person, librarianship is the right choice.

But does it provide a life-long challenge? After a dozen years at the cataloging station or the reference desk, does it provide daily satisfaction, and will it do so over the years ahead? Once again this is a realistic condition of library work that should be remembered by the personnel administrator. Attention should be given not only to the fresh recruit but also to the apathetic veteran. Continued motivation of the professional on the plateau is another of the challenges for the personnel administrator.

FUTURE OF THE LIBRARIAN

What is the prospect for the 21st century? The crystal ball is not clear. The positive factors in the career of the librarian are likely to continue: the appeal of the work, satisfaction on the job, association with other like-minded professionals, serving inquirers seeking knowledge. Some of the detriments, such as low salaries and uncertain image, may improve to some degree, but any improvement will occur slowly. The larger question concerns changes that will probably occur outside libraries that may affect not only the institution but also the profession.

Education in general is being scrutinized and criticized at the present time. Presidential campaigns have devoted considerable attention to the topic, and while sometimes conflicting remedies have been proposed, there is agreement on the need for improvement. In a recent campaign one presidential candidate called the educational system a "mess," and the two other candidates had definite platforms for change. The "Education President" was defeated in the last presidential election, not because he adopted the label but in part because he failed to live up to the claim.

Condemnation of our schools has become widely fashionable. People refer to high-school graduates who can't read or write. Actually the United States has many effective schools and our college population has moved steadily upward in numbers if community colleges are included in the count. What has happened is that poverty has spread in the inner cities. When poverty increases, family life is weakened, and when families break down more and more children come to school with neither the background nor the discipline required for formal learning. Don't blame the schools for shortcomings in other parts of the society.

One of the solutions frequently suggested is a "voucher" system, whereby each youngster would be given a credit to cover part of the cost of attendance at a school of choice, including private and parochial institutions. This, it is said, will set up competition that will improve education. Actually this will drain money away from public schools, particularly those in the inner cities, as some students take their vouchers and go elsewhere, leaving the weaker schools with less state aid. It will also segregate schools along racial lines because more of the Caucasion youngsters will be able to take advantage of the vouchers, which will cover only part of the cost at a distant school. (Could this re-segregation be the reason that some people advocate vouchers?) The result will be more schools, smaller schools, and the remarkable institution of the American public school will be weakened.

Among the casualties of the many smaller schools are likely to be librarians—and libraries. If some such reform takes hold, the future of school librarianship will be definitely set back. The school library in many instances will become the book room or book closet of the past, with part-time or volunteer help or with a teacher in charge for a few hours a week.

Furthermore, continued recession in the economy will adversely affect libraries across the board. The starting point is to get the American economy healthy again, after which progress can be resumed in public, academic, special and school libraries. Without this, budgets will be cut, hours reduced, jobs sacrificed. Even as libraries grew with the country as it became a super economic power, so they will decline if the country cannot regain vigor and confidence.

Then there are the technological changes that will occur in these next years. Depending on how this develops, and depending on how librarians react, technological change could be the most uncertain and fundamental force on libraries in the future. So important is this prospect that the final chapter in the present volume is devoted to its implications.

The librarian has emerged and is fairly-well established. Will the librarian flourish or decline in the next years? The answer depends in part on the quality and foresight of personnel administration.

REFERENCES

1. Edward A. Parsons, *The Alexandrian Library* (New York: American Elsevier Publishing Co., 1952), 136.
2. James W. Thompson, *The Medieval Library* (New York: Hafner, 1957), 615.
3. *Ibid.*, 619.

4. Josephine M. Smith, *A Chronology of Librarianship* (Metuchen, NJ: Scarecrow Press, 1968), 63.
5. Jesse H. Shera, *Foundations of the Public Library* (Chicago: University of Chicago Press, 1948), 163.
6. Charles C. Williamson, *Training for Library Service* (Boston: Merrymount Press, 1923).

3. HUMAN RELATIONS IN PERSONNEL ADMINISTRATION

A revolution in the theory of managing workers has occurred over the last century. The new approach, usually known as human relations, is based on findings in behavioral science. The term may be too inclusive. Library catalogs use the human relations heading for everything from making friends to winning arguments, but our interest here is in human relations in the workplace.

In this context, the term refers to emphasis on workers—their motivations, needs, interests and satisfactions. And it usually takes a positive viewpoint of human nature.

Most enlightened administrators incline toward the new theory, say that they practice human relations, and in most cases sincerely believe that they do so. But in reality some of these managers—including some in the library field—fall back on the older autocratic method when the going gets tough. Just when they should be drawing on the strength of the staff, they revert to centralized decision making and the issuing of directives. Human relations may be all well and good, according to this view, when we are going along as a happy family, but comes a severe budget crunch or mounting criticism from users or a sharp decline in staff morale, and the old ways come to the fore. The administrator, under pressure, concludes that action, not consultation, is what is needed.

Human relations has become a platitude of personnel administration; most textbooks and seminars subscribe to it. But the remarkable thing is that human relations—for all its support and prevalence—is often not practiced.

Either overtly or in more subtle forms, the old approach of boss and worker, those who order and those who obey, creeps back into the relationship. Many a personnel administrator gives lip service to the concept and then turns to deal with problems that have been caused by lack of constructive human relations, whether problems of productivity, of internal friction, of indifference and morale.

This book, therefore, starts with a review of the new trend in management, the emergence of human relations in the workplace, and then goes on to a hard-headed look at why it is often violated or overlooked in practice. With this background in hand, we can then get down to the business of acquiring staff, training workers, evaluating performance, motivating employees, and getting the work of the agency done.

OLD-FASHIONED AUTOCRATIC CONTROL

The traditional view of administration of personnel was that of the boss and the worker, the supervisor and the supervised. Henry Ford got it all into one sentence: "Just set the work before the men and have them do it." This approach produced the Model T and in time almost brought the Ford Motor Company to bankruptcy. Employees were told what to do, were watched to see that they did it, and were disciplined or even dismissed if they did not. Orders, control and discipline made the enterprise function.

In this environment, workers did what they had to do, and very little more. There was little commitment and less enthusiasm. Moral was neither good nor bad; it hardly existed at all. Employees kept an eye on the time clock, and sought satisfaction off the job.

The prevailing mode of administration during the 19th century and well into the 20th was autocratic. Democracy prevailed in the body politic but not in the workplace. This was true not just in burgeoning industry but also in burgeoning government and service institutions.

Decisions were made at the top and passed down

through the ranks. Workers had no choice except to accept conditions and methods and salaries, no matter how arbitrary. At that time, employees in factories and offices accepted this relationship. Their aim was straightforward, to get a start in the expanding American economy, which they achieved with a regular paycheck and reasonable job security. The thought that workers might expect some personal satisfaction from their many hours on the job, much less that they had any contribution to make to how the job was organized, did not enter the picture.

Even in libraries autocratic administration was common. Reference to the biography of Herbert Putnam, the great Librarian of Congress from 1899 to 1939, shows a man who issued orders and had limited relations with his staff. He was characterized as "aloof, remote, detached."[1] It is said that he rode up in the staff elevator each morning knowing that the others on the elevator were library employees, but never once said "Good morning." Yet he is credited with leading the Library of Congress from a limited role to that of National Library.

Carl Roden, the scholarly Director of the Chicago Public Library from 1925 to 1950, is another example. He called the tune from the front office and remained remote from the staff. He was followed by Gertrude Gscheidle, another autocrat, who told employees what to do in no uncertain terms, and then tried the same tactic on the City Council, which lost her the support of her own Board of Directors. One morning she took her purse out of the bottom drawer and went to City Hall and put in for her pension, thus ending a distinguished career.

NEW-FASHIONED HUMAN RELATIONS

In contrast, the concept of human relations has emerged over the past half-century or more, and has come to be the prevailing theory. The worker is to be seen as a human being, the purposes of the organization and the purposes of the individual are to be brought together. Workers, according to this theory, will respond and dedicate themselves to the enterprise, work will get done, cooperation among individuals will occur. Staff members will get personal satisfaction on the job, not just when they leave the workplace. And they will be able to contribute to planning and decision making.

Scientific Management

The story starts, oddly enough, with a man who depended on a stopwatch and time and motion study. In the early 1900s, Frederick Taylor studied men shoveling coal and engaged in other physical work, and developed the most productive motions and the best tools for the jobs. He analyzed the best organization of tasks, convenience of the workplace, and coordinated assembling of the materials needed. Based on such data, he established standards of productivity for the various tasks—number of tons of coal that should be shoveled in a day, for example. Taylor termed his approach "Scientific Management."[2]

What has this to do with human relations? From present perspectives it is clear that workers were looked at mechanically; they were in a sense to become robots, and this led not long afterward to Henry Ford's assembly line. Remember Charlie Chaplin in *Modern Times?* The criterion was efficiency, productivity.

Other applications were made of scientific management. The Gilbreths, Frank and Lillian,[3] designed convenient and efficient kitchens, which were a particular boon to older and handicapped people. We see the heritage of that today in the well-designed kitchen, with the work counter between the sink on one side and the stove on the other, and with bowls and plates in adjacent overhead cabinets. Efficient, "scientific" organization of work stations applies even in libraries, from the arrangement of the librarian's desk in a one-person library to the set-up at the charge-out desk in larger agencies.

Scientific management had an impact on the worker-supervisor relationship. Taylor shifted the focus from autocratic, arbitrary supervision to workers themselves and the best plan to facilitate their endeavors. This also opened the possibility of ideas for improvement coming upward from the individual employee. He pushed his point by stressing that efficiency led to greater production and thence to greater profits, in which workers could (theoretically) share in the form of better salaries.

In other words, the human being entered the equation. And the task of the personnel administrator was thereby changed, from boss to facilitator.

Hawthorne Experiments

The next step forward came with the famous Hawthorne experiments of Elton Mayo in the 1920s, at a plant of the Western Electric Company.[4] Social scientists from Harvard University were brought into the factory to see if adjustments in working conditions made any difference in productivity. While some experiments worked out as anticipated, other results were unexpected and at first were hard to interpret. One series of experiments involved providing more rest periods and schedule flexibility for workers at manual tasks.

As expected, production did go up with more liberal provisions. But, oddly enough, performance still remained high when schedules were cut back to the previous level. How to account for this positive response under adverse conditions? Another series of experiments dealt with lighting at the work station. Lighting was improved, shadows and glare were eliminated, and—again as expected—productivity increased. But the researchers were hard-headed and proceeded to cut illumination back to the earlier level. Once again productivity remained high. The researchers puzzled over these results.

Interviews with the workers brought out the fact that their morale was raised by the experiments because individuals felt important as a result of the attention being given to them. When the lighting was decreased, for example, the workers said they noted the difference but thought the experimenters were rather dumb in their understanding of illumination; the employees kept up their high productivity because they felt that the researchers were really trying to improve conditions. It was how the workers felt about the attention paid to them that resulted in their performance, and not the objective changes that had influenced them.

Such experiments again turned the focus toward the interrelations between supervisors and workers. People responded to efforts to improve the work environment. Psychological and social factors thus came into play.

Two results were clear from the Hawthorne experiments, both bearing on human relations. First, the attitude of management toward workers is more important than physical conditions in promoting productivity. Second, the influence of co-workers, peer pressure on the job, played a definite role in how employees responded. The worker as human being was moved to center stage for study.

But it soon became apparent that human relations were more complex than such simple experiments indicated. The panacea was not simple manipulation of work schedules or physical conditions or similar objective factors. Indeed, some efforts at such manipulation soon backfired, with workers concluding that management was playing games with them. Human relations were important, but only when the total spectrum of reactions of employees was taken into account. The personnel manager had to know the full range of behavioral science as manifested in the work situation.

The Hawthorne experiments, and similar research in the following years, indicated that workers were seeking something more from employment than the salary check. Somehow the job had to give them personal satisfaction beyond the pay envelope. But how could employment make for productivity and at the same time serve the personal needs of workers? Were not the two antithetical, with companies and institutions seeking profits and service, while the workers were now seeking personal satisfaction on the job. The picture was complex; answers did not come easily. Nor did performance during World War II simplify the problem. Both factory workers and office workers—as well as the men and women in uniform—

rose to the challenge of the War and made a notable contribution. It was clear that they believed in the cause and therefore made an extraordinary effort. Attention shifted further from efficiency to human nature, and particularly to the motivation of workers.

But what exactly did the worker want and expect? Obviously we could not wait for another war to get maximum production. Were there ways to get that same effort in normal times? This is the question that faced the post-war years.

To this point we have reviewed three successive stages in twentieth-century personnel administration—from autocratic control to scientific organization of jobs, to recognition of workers on the job. But the nature of the psychological factors being uncovered was still obscure and little understood. If workers were seeking something other than a salary check and reasonable working conditions, what were these additional expectations and motivators?

Human Relations Theory

Enter the behavioral scientists, the human relations specialists. From backgrounds in psychology and sociology, behavioral scientists sought to explain the influences and dynamics of the workplace and the worker. The literature issued on the subject after World War II is voluminous, and only a few highlights can be summarized here.

Douglas McGregor introduced Theory X and Theory Y.[5] The first stood for old-line management, with close control, orders from above, and the worker as a cog in a machine. Theory Y rested on a positive view of human nature: average human beings do not dislike work, they are prepared to accept a measure of responsibility and even have a capacity for ingenuity and creativity, and thus will exercise self-direction and self-control and gain satisfaction from dedication to the objectives of the organization for which they work.

One wonders about this rosy scenario. While there are positions devoted to very useful products and to constructive purposes, there are many more where the results are less than noble and heroic. The skeptic can ask whether all this satisfaction can come about from the making of toothpaste or the digging of ditches or serving as a prison guard.

But certainly there are some workers who exemplify McGregor's benign viewpoint. School teachers would be one example. They must share the objectives of the institution or they would not be in the school; they do their best without much supervision, and at least some go home with a feeling of accomplishment. And good teachers may be among the most valuable workers in the society.

Frederick Hertzberg[6] carried the analysis a step further. He separated "hygiene factors" and "motivation factors." The former include salary and working conditions, which must be at a reasonable level or morale will suffer. But these factors alone do not insure dedication and enthusiasm among workers. The second group, motivational factors—sense of achievement, recognition for work well done, opportunity for advancement—he sees as the source of high morale and extra effort beyond the call of duty.

Abraham Maslow probed deeper and came up with a sequence of five levels of personal motivation.[7] The factors workers seek, in his view, can be grouped in these five successive steps:

1. Physiological needs (warmth, space, air)
2. Safety factors (freedom from accidents and threats to health)
3. Group feeling (sense of identification, of belonging)
4. Ego needs (recognition, feeling of importance)
5. Self-fullfilment (realization of personal goals)

As each step is achieved, the worker looks for the next higher level. The job that fulfills all five levels would have the fullest possible contribution from the individual. This formulation has had relatively wide acceptance, and has for the most part stood up under investigation.

Implications of Human Relations

In recent years the literature emphasizes two factors that grow out of Theory Y and considerations of motivation: participation and careers. Work these out and you will be well along toward a productive and creative staff. The worker is to be drawn into the enterprise rather than be treated as a piece of equipment in human form. And provision is to be made for a career to which the worker can aspire. Both of these are motivating factors, but they pose serious problems in many enterprises.

Reaching down and drawing in middle management is not too difficult to achieve. Some firms have a kind of general cabinet including department heads and intermediate managers who sit from time to time with the top brass and review progress and problems. Many firms naturally turn to a department head when an issue arises that involves the department. But reaching below that, to workers on the line, whether professional-technical or clerical-supportive, is much less common. Top management may see little benefit from such consultation and begrudge the time involved. To include the total staff in planning sessions requires a change in management attitude, from a hard-headed "let's dispose of this problem" approach to an appreciation of the input that may come form anywhere down the line, and an appreciation of the human dividend that results when individuals feel that their opinions are important.

Some such change in attitude is occurring in business, albeit slowly. It is interesting to note that the Ford Motor Co., adopting the slogan "Quality Is Job 1" to counter the charge of lack of reliability in American automobiles, chooses to demonstrate this in advertising by featuring individual workers on the assembly line. It is not the boss but the worker who is to convey the image of quality. One hopes that this is not just advertising, that administrators have actually learned to listen to the man or woman who can identify a problem and suggest what to do about it.

Another way that workers are being drawn in is by

means of teams assigned to a group of tasks. Rather than
doing one isolated job, the individual participates as a
member of a work group, exchanging tasks with co-
workers and making a contribution to how the team
should operate. You don't just talk to yourself but to
others, and then together make what arrangements and
adjustments are necessary. One listing of actions which
work teams in the factory do includes the following:

    −rotate as leaders of teams
    −handle all quality control
    −handle housekeeping
    −are responsible for safety
    −have access to all tools
    −help determine staffing levels

All these are tasks formerly handled by supervisors.[8]

Building in career opportunities is another factor
stressed in recent research. Promising career prospects are
built into the management ranks but are more difficult to
achieve for the worker on the line. Supervisors have a
more complex job in the era of human relations administration, and they should be suitably rewarded for their
contribution. This is a promotion to which the worker in
the factory or in the office can aspire. Shortly, attention
will be given to how career prospects can be worked out in
libraries, for support staff as well as professionals.

Also growing out of recent research is increased recognition of the influence of social groups within a staff
group. We saw that phenomenon way back in the Hawthorne experiments, where the workers as a group responded positively to efforts to improve their working
conditions and put pressure on any skeptical individuals
to go along. Of course the group pressure may also be
negative, spreading antagonism and opposition through
the system.

There is an equation or balance in personnel administration: individuals on the one side, social systems within
the workplace on the other. Part of the responsibility of
the personnel manager is to make the two function to-

gether, a by-no-means simple balancing act. How the balance is maintained goes a long way toward determining both the satisfaction of the individual worker and the success of the organization.

Strongly motivated recruits may come to the library and find an organization with unclear purposes, vague standards and weak administration. Which will prevail is problematical. As likely as not, the ongoing enterprise may frustrate the recruits, wearing away their resolve. Staff members will conclude that this is only a job, to be done with a minimum of effort and dedication.

Conversely, a positive and cooperative organization can be weakened by an influx of persons seeking a soft job. A social structure can take in and convert just so much dead wood before losing its vigor and resiliency.

Of course, individuals and work groups are not opposites, not distinct and separate forces. The individuals are the group; together they constitute the social system. If the individual workers have a strong sense of purpose, so does the staff as a whole. If the organization is alert and cooperative and dedicated, this means that the units within it display these qualities. The two reinforce each other.

So personnel administrators must be psychologists on the one hand and sociologists on the other. In one hour they deal with personal problems, seeking to find out why a staff member has turned glum and unfriendly, and in the next hour with the whole group, seeking to convince the staff of the need for greater use of automated data bases. The manager should not just think of individuals and their performance, but also of trends and the worries and hopes of all or many staff members as a group.

Sometimes a clique within the group can determine the attitude which the whole group adopts. Some questionable gripes are brought forward by the group. Young people are being too disruptive in the library, they may say; old people are asking for too much assistance; the evening hours are not worth staying open because of low attendance; morning hours are being usurped by loafers. The supervisor, hearing these group views, and then talking to individual staff members, may be surprised to learn that some members really do not support these positions, but have just been going along with the crowd. Of course, all this may go the other way: the group may push for an improvement in service—whether books reshelved more promptly or greater depth in subject analysis of new acquisitions. Where the social system is moving in positive directions, managers can only encourage the process.

Where the opposite is true, managers have several options. The whole group might be confronted to see if persuasion can defuse the negative view. Or an effort might be made to mobilize those who do not go along with the group view, in the hope that they may win over adherents to their position. Or a task force with members from both sides might be set up in order to give thorough consideration to the various viewpoints. The latter course of action would normally be preferred because it gives recognition to both sides and provides a fair chance that the merit in both positions can be given attention. The result may bring about a balance between individual and group views.

The human relations theme persists in the recent literature. One variation uses the term "the worth ethic." This author concludes: "You need the human heart at work."[9]

THE JAPANESE MODEL

A brief examination of the much-vaunted Japanese methods for personnel administration may add to an understanding of methods in the United States. While systems cannot be automatically transferred between countries, because of different traditions and cultures, there is a lesson to be learned from the Japanese experience.

A superficial understanding of Japanese methods tends to concentrate on bits and pieces that are unusual, such as the lifetime employment provided for workers. But the differences go deeper and therefore have more far-reaching effect. The very conception of the capitalistic enterprise in Japan contrasts with the American perception. In our country the shareholders and the capital investors are seen as the crucial element in the enterprise, and profit is seen as the corporate goal. If profits are down or losses occur, the shareholders and, to some extent, management remain, while workers are fired or laid off. The core is the capital and the buildings and tools and processes which capital makes possible.

In Japan, by contrast, the human resources are put foremost. Emphasis is on the "human capital" of the enterprise as its most precious resource, and not on finance or equipment. Money capital in Japan comes primarily from institutional investors and bank credits rather than from individual share holders. Dividends are relatively low in Japan. If profits occur they are shared by management and workers in the form of bonuses; if losses occur they too are shared by the total staff.

Following from this conception of corporate enterprise, personnel policies and administration are built up from the individual worker, not passed down from the board room. Management and employees see themselves as united in carrying the enterprise forward. From this there follows such distinctive features as internalized labor practices, decentralized decision making, and participative management. One author has called this "human capitalism."[10] The result is to move higher on Maslow's levels of needs, to self-esteem and sense of accomplishment for the worker.

Each of these practices will be examined more thoroughly in succeeding chapters, but they are explained briefly here so that the Japanese model can be more fully understood.

In Japan the work force is seen as a group or society. Employees join the group, usually for life, knowing that careers will be provided and promotions will occur from within. It is an internalized labor market, as contrasted with the American practice of laying off workers in hard times and filling high-level positions with specialists from outside.

The members of the labor group are seen as dedicated

and intelligent workers who have a contribution to make to the analysis of problems and the making of decisions. Considerable effort is devoted to training and retraining of workers. One of the standard practices is to have a bell or a cord at each work station which the employee can use to call attention to any lack of quality or other shortcoming in the fabricating process. When a defect is noted—say in a automobile under assembly—the cord is pulled, the supervisor steps in, and either the assembly line is stopped and the defect corrected immediately or a note is made for the correction to be made at the end of the line.

Workers are trained not in one specific task but in related activities, so they can serve as members of teams and rotate tasks. Day-to-day decisions are made by groups of employees on the job, and not as much by means of centralized regulations and supervisors' directions. In this humanistic system, with long-term employment, innovation and change are welcomed and not opposed by workers, because they know they will not be displaced, and also know that if innovation is encouraged the firm will progress. Actually, many fresh ideas come up from the workplace. Because the emphasis is on human resources, the firm provides health care, subsidized housing, cultural and educational programs, and recreational facilities. All this contrasts with the usual American pattern of centralized direction.

But the Japanese model is not without problems and weaknesses. Labor unions complain that the employee is under pressure and may be overworked. Neither women nor minorities are treated well under the system. As competition mounts, whether internal or international, it may not be possible to guarantee life-time employment. And there is no question that basic management decisions are made at the top, not by a consensus of employees.

Can the Japanese system of human capitalism be applied to America's traditional capitalism? Perhaps, but there are many roadblocks in the way. The change would involve not just the adoption of certain practices and techniques, but actually a change in conception and understanding of the economic system. Further, the

American model is deeply imbedded. Any fundamental change would run into opposition from investors, from management and from labor unions, and might even be challenged as communistic, even though human capitalism is the exact opposite of communism with its central government control.

What has occurred in America, and what may continue to occur, is utilization of pieces of the Japanese plan, such as working teams and suggestion boxes. The piecemeal adoptions to date have produced mixed results and have not had a pronounced impact strong enough to stimulate broad-scale adjustment on the part of American industry. In the case of Japanese firms that have set up plants in the United States—Honda, Nummi, Nissan and Toyota—American workers have generally been satisfied with their working conditions and have resisted efforts of unions to organize them.[11] Workers in these plants feel that the humanistic personnel practices upgrade their status.

Does the Japanese system have any application to libraries? Here the prospect is more hopeful, because libraries do not have some of the built-in characteristics of industry. There are no investors looking for immediate profits, library managers have usually come out of the ranks of practicing librarians, and the work itself offers more opportunity for personal satisfaction. It is not too much to say that library work comes closer to "human capitalism" than employment in most manufacturing operations. Worker-centered supervision will permeate the following pages on personnel administration in libraries.

QUESTIONS ABOUT HUMAN RELATIONS

The human relations school rests upon a very optimistic view of human nature. It is assumed that people are prepared to work and want to work. They are prepared to expend reasonable effort if they believe they are respected and treated fairly. Under these circumstances they need minimum supervision because they are self-motivated. Further, they are disposed to be loyal to the purposes of their employing agency, taking pride in its success. Salaries should be adequate and competitive, but their primary motivation comes from a sense of work well done and a feeling that their effort is recognized.

But do the psychological theories take account of the wide variety of humankind? I remember a lesson I learned very early in my career. I was a part-time book shelver in a busy branch library in Chicago. After a period, I was given a chance to shift during slack periods to checking in magazines received in the mail, which I welcomed both for the variety and the little extra responsibility. When the branch became extra busy another book shelver was hired and I was asked to keep track of his work as a kind of supervisor. He proved to be a steady if not very fast performer. In an effort to motivate him a little more, I brought him into the magazine checking activity in order to give him the variety that I had welcomed. He evidently recognized what I was doing and shortly told me that there was no need for the adjustment, that he was perfectly content to plug along on shelving books. I learned not to project my own interests and wishes on others.

We all know individuals with one set of motivations and others with an opposite set. David Riesman warned of this variety and diversity,[12] and postulated three different sets of drives and satisfaction among people. Some are tradition-directed, relying primarily on custom, myths and taboos as the determining factors in personality and conduct. A second group is inner-directed, relying on values and beliefs inculcated over the years and held to tenaciously. Finally, a large group is other-directed, acting on the approval or disapproval of others. Would all three groups react uniformly to any set of working conditions?

Supervisors who have had subordinates who remained indifferent, who would give the minimum required but no more, who tried to get away with as much as possible, contest the benign view of human nature. There may be floaters and malingerers in any group of employees. However, in such instances the total conditions of the job, the methods of selection and orientation of staff, and the nature of the supervision itself would have to be examined before blame could be assigned, whether to the individuals or the administration.

Salary not a motivating factor? This also flies in the face of experience. A recent television program provided a portrait of the Lincoln Electric Co. in Cleveland. The firm provides a minimum of fringe benefits and very little of human relations supervision, yet has no trouble getting employees. They simply provide salary levels $10,000 or more per year above the competition, and workers respond and work hard. Is desire for material reward really gone?

Wall Street has a related but different objection. From the standpoint of business, the shift to behavioral considerations is a kind of challenge of the profit motive. *Fortune* magazine has been critical of what it calls the "social engineers." One advocate of this view put it this way: "To say, in fact, that the American worker is not really or primarily interested in money contradicts, in a deep sense, the very motive power of the economic system."[13] Such a comment prompts librarians to wonder about their own motives. Surely it was not expectation of substantial monetary rewards that got them into the profession.

Other questions can be raised about human relations theory in the workplace. Drawing workers into decision-making? Individual employees seldom know the complete picture of resources, budgets and problems. They are likely to propose solutions suitable to their particular part of the enterprise, and in any case will not have responsibility for whatever action is taken. And isn't it true that many subordinates "play it safe" and hesitate to oppose the views of those in charge?

The time comes when the buck stops in the front office, and the final decision will have to be made there. Indeed, strong leadership, particularly when an enterprise faces radical change or restructuring, or adoption of a new goal, can result in centralized administration—and it may work, assuming that staff down the line believe in and share in the new program.

Some managers have studied the new psychological theories and then sought to apply them in order to manipulate subordinates. This may work for a time, but then workers can see through the tricks. Of course, misuse of a theory does not prove that it is wrong.

The voice that has reached the widest audience, in both business and service circles, is Peter Drucker's. He has been writer, lecturer, teacher and consultant. Recently he applied his fresh and independent outlook to service enterprises, in a book warmly recommended to library administrators.[14] Cutting through the various theories, Drucker stresses two elements of administration: clarification of objectives and measurement of results. He would use objectives as the basis for organization. Rather than a structure focused on function (cataloging, reference, etc.), he would start with an "education" unit in the public library and a "research" unit in the university library. Staff would be recruited expressly to serve these objectives, jobs would be defined by them, collections built for the same purpose—and results determined in relation to the objective that was set. He is sympathetic to the human relations school, but puts the focus on responsibility on the part of workers.

The reader, confused and uncertain about the various psychological theories of worker motivation, would do well to turn to Peter Drucker for clarification and balance. And the wise administrator would do well to apply the human relations doctrine as far as possible, while recognizing the infinite variety of human nature and also the ultimate responsibility of the administrator.

APPLICATION TO LIBRARIES

How does all this apply to libraries? Could it be that libraries are so humanely administered that there is no need to study the human relations movement? Or do library administrators subscribe to the movement while politely and subtly practicing autocratic personnel management?

Neither question as it stands can be answered categorically yes or no. Certainly libraries are not run like 19th-century factories or present-day sweatshops. On the other hand, few libraries have realized and utilized the full potential of their staffs. And then, of course, there are the variations, positive and negative, from agency to agency. There are authoritarian managers in the library ranks, there are those who respect and capitalize on staff members' interests, knowledge and needs, and there are many in between.

By and large libraries provide ground for positive human relations. In general, libraries attract workers who are sympathetic to the purposes of the institution. Certainly this applies to professionals, who have consciously chosen librarianship, and to some extent to clericals, who believe that libraries are pleasant places in which to work. They were not particularly attracted by salaries, for the agency is not strong in financial rewards.

Further, many staff members are well educated, so they can readily grasp and appreciate the library's opportunities and accomplishments. There is experience and expertise in the ranks that is not always evident to managers: the cataloger becomes conscious of an inconsistency in the catalog, the reference librarian is the first to note requests for material not in the collection, the children's librarian realizes that some of the children do not have English as a first language, the desk attendant notes that part of the transaction process takes an undue amount of time. Each is in a position to call attention to needs and problems, and each has something to contribute to solutions. Because of the non-coercive and cooperative environment that prevails in some libraries, an exchange of information and joint solution of problems occurs. The result is that the library improves, the manager disposes of a problem, and the individual staff member has a sense of satisfaction as part of the team.

But many libraries do not take advantage of this opportunity. This is not necessarily because the head librarian and the department heads are outright autocrats in their style, although this does occur. The main reason for lack of full human relations benefits is that many library managers and supervisors are passive administrators.

They don't dictate to staff, nor do they watch over them too closely; but equally, they do not bring staff actively into planning, do not encourage staff to watch for problems, report needs, help in deciding what to do. Not negative, not authoritarian, but passive.

Libraries by their nature are orderly, tranquil places. The hum of activity is subdued. Administrators want the agency to run smoothly and on a straight course; they would prefer that problems not be emphasized, they would like to avoid change. Sometimes these attitudes are conscious, but often they are subconscious. Many managers would sincerely object if charged with being passive. Without analyzing their attitudes, they would like the agency to be steady, relaxed and friendly.

Staff members, from their side, get the message and do not stir up the waters. Steady as she goes. A kind of benign autocracy prevails. Workers, finding few challenges, go about their jobs and occasionally wonder why the appeal and sense of accomplishment are gone. Then, when the time for change comes, either expansion or retrenchment, the staff tends to resist, for they have become accustomed to passive supervision and the steady course.

We are familiar with criticisms of the performance of government agencies, carried regularly in newspapers and other media. Reduction of government inefficiency and ineffectiveness are watchwords of presidential campaigns. Even the public schools have come in for repeated censure, along with proposals for alternative schools.

A recent newspaper account[15] tells of a sharp turn-around in the cutting of trees by government crews in New York City. Given the threat of shifting the cutting to private firms, the park employees requested and received permission to plan "their own routes, schedules and workloads," and promptly lowered the cost per tree to less than the outside firms would charge. Perhaps this was the result of changes in routes and schedules, but more likely the government crews simply worked harder as a result of being granted control over their work conditions.

The task before us is to see how human relations can be incorporated into the various aspects of personnel administration in libraries. The goal in these pages is how library and administrators can develop staff groups that are (1) trained, (2) dedicated, (3) motivated, (4) productive, (5) participative, (6) satisfied, and (7) receptive to change. A tall order.

REFERENCES

1. Charles A. Goodrum, and Helen W. Dalrymple, *The Library of Congress* (Boulder, CO: Westview Press, 1982), 33.
2. Frederick W. Taylor, *The Principles of Scientific Management* (New York: Harper, 1911).
3. Frank B., Gilbreth, Jr. and Ernestine Gilbreth Casey. *Cheaper by the Dozen* (New York: Crowell, 1948).
4. Elton Mayo, *The Human Problems of an Industrial Civilization* (Cambridge, MA: Harvard University Press, 1933); and F.J. Roethlisberger, and W.J. Dickson, *Management and the Worker* (Cambridge, MA: Harvard University Press, 1939).
5. Douglas McGregor, *The Human Side of Enterprise* (New York: McGraw-Hill, 1960).
6. Frederick Herzberg, *The Motivation to Work* (New York: Wiley, 1959).
7. Abraham Maslow, *Motivation and Personality* (New York: Harper and Row, 1970).
8. Tom Peters, *Thriving on Chaos* (New York: Knopf, 1987), 291.
9. Kate Ludeman, *The Worth Ethic* (New York: Dutton, 1989), XI.
10. Robert Ozaki, *Human Capitalism* (Tokyo: Kodaush International, 1991).
11. Robert Ozaki, *Ibid.*, 173–174.
12. David Riesman, *The Lonely Crowd* (New Haven, CT: Yale University Press, 1950).
13. Daniel Bell, *Work and Its Discontents* (Boston: Beacon Press, 1965), 29.
14. Peter F. Drucker, *Managing the Non-Profit Organization: Practices and Principles* (New York: HarperCollins, 1990).
15. *New York Times,* November 16, 1992, B12.

4. GETTING ORGANIZED: POSITION CLASSIFICATION AND SALARIES

Before hiring staff, an enterprise has to get organized. Even in the simplest of tasks confronting a group—digging a ditch or moving a book collection—there needs to be a supervisor (official or unofficial), separate jobs, assignment of individuals to jobs, and a system of rewards. If these conditions do not exist, if every member of the group starts doing his/her own thing, after a period of confusion someone is likely to say, "Wait a minute, let's get organized." In larger and more complex enterprises, a structure of positions and relationships builds up and we call this "organization." Another volume in this series has examined organization in libraries: *Organizational Structure of Libraries,* 1984.

Certain aspects of organization apply particularly to personnel administration and need to be reviewed here. At the outset, identification of tasks and jobs is needed, and then a combination of these jobs into a position classification plan. This disposes workers to their place in the organization, where all can make their contribution. Salaries for groups of positions must be established. Only then is an agency ready to find and hire staff, and only then are potential candidates in a position to determine whether they are interested or not. You have to organize the team before you go on the field.

THE ORGANIZATIONAL HIERARCHY

Over the years, as the sizes and kinds of group enterprises have increased, the predominant structure of organization that has evolved is the hierarchy of command, from chief officer down to individual worker, often with many levels between. This is typically pictured in an organization chart that takes the shape of a pyramid. Individual jobs fit somewhere in the pyramid, with a supervisor of some kind above each worker. At the top is the C.E.O., the director, and head librarian.

This typical model of personnel administration emerged before and after the turn of the century. Early in the 1900s, Max Weber analyzed the growing industrial and governmental enterprises of the time.[1] He described their structure as "bureaucracy," meaning a multi-layered pyramid of command that held the enterprise together and got its work done. He admired the way the total task could be broken down into individual jobs, and workers with different skills and levels of competence recruited into these slots. The manager had a structure which could convey his directives, and workers had a place in which they belonged.

But bureaucracy carried the seeds of its own weakness. Communication of any kind—from managers, from workers, from customers—had to move through several levels, in the course of which it could become confused and even lost. Individual workers on their side were isolated in a particular niche and had little conception of the total enterprise and its overall goals. Thus the bureaucracy which our political candidates promise to remedy, at least at election time.

Henri Fayol added to the rationalization for the system. From his background in mining, he saw that bureaucracy could miss its mark. His remedy: planning and control. He prescribed Authority, Discipline, Unity of Command.[2] Hard-headed administrators adopted his ideas and ran a "tight ship."

Thus we had the model of the "top-down" organization, with centralized control, a goodly contingent of sergeants and supervisors, and the troops marching neatly in a row. Authority and control would get work done.

Fayol's work was carried forward by Luther Gulick in the 1930s. His background was in government and the administrative problems of the huge expansion in agencies in Washington to meet the Great Depression. Gulick set forth a "science of administration."[3] Working within the bureaucratic model, he stressed unity of command, span of control, use of staff as well as line officers, and departmental structure by purpose, process, clientele, or geographic location. These concepts were described as "principles" and were taught in universities and management seminars. All had been neatly reduced to a science.

Gulick held to the view that close control was the way to make enterprises work. Actually this concept contributed to bureaucracy in the negative sense. Applying his principle of narrow span of control, administrators added layer after layer to the pyramid of organization, and in time both the goals and the responsiveness of service agencies were blunted. Understanding of structure, following of channels were to be the solution, not the understanding of human nature.

Thus, by mid-century, a body of administrative theory existed, covering all aspects of enterprises from their chain of command to the physical motions of the individual worker. The complexities of organizations of workers had been reduced to a machine. The administrator had only to study the individual parts and then the principles of how the parts related to each other, and productivity and profits and service would surely result.

The only catch was that organizations of people do not function like machines. There are factors within the organization that work against mechanical efficiency. The individuality of people does not always fit the prescribed patterns. The real world of group enterprise was not the same as the body of theory.

To begin with, groups of workers—whether in the factory or in the government office or in the library—were seeking more than command and control in the job. The human relations trend and the work of behavioral scientists showed that individuals more and more sought recognition, a sense of purpose and a sense of accomplishment in the workplace. If they found these satisfactions they were prepared to offer motivation, dedication, loyalty and constructive ideas in return. If the satisfactions are lacking, they pull back and do only what is specifically assigned.

Within the "top-down," authoritative structure these qualities are not easy to attain. Individual workers are isolated and too far from the aims and objectives of the enterprise to readily develop dedication. Furthermore, the workers cannot see how their own efforts relate to those of others, and therefore cannot coordinate with the larger activity. Communication coming down to them can be distorted as it moves through the many levels, and their own ideas get lost in moving up the pyramid. They pull back into their own departments and their individual jobs, which become ends in themselves—hence the poor service we often experience at a government office.

So-called "staff" officers also affect the neat pattern based on the principle of unity of command. Such officers include financial or legal and even personnel specialists. Theoretically they have only an advisory capacity, with control left in the hands of the "line" officer such as a department head or group supervisor. An example at the federal level is the Office of Management and Budget, which is supposed to provide only financial information and advice, but which in practice may directly influence budget allocations, and therefore the programs of the operating agencies. In the library field a different kind of example would be the Coordinator of Children's Services in a large public library. The head of a branch library is in charge of what goes on in the branch, yet the children's program promulgated by the central Coordinator may determine the activity of an important part of the branch unit.

Perhaps the most serious charge that can be brought against the traditional bureaucratic organization is that it resists change, inhibits adjustment to new goals and opportunities. The hierarchy is a means of control, not a means of adjustment. Individual workers are in their compartments and have difficulty seeing the larger picture. Middle managers are expected to keep the enterprise on course, not to search out alternative programs. Ideas for change readily get lost in the hierarchy. Note the problem of employees who see something wrong and speak out; "whistle blowers" do not have an easy time. This resistance to change is a matter of concern to libraries as they seek to meet the challenge of new ways of transmitting ideas and information.

Beyond all these factors within an organization, there are outside strictures and influences which also may affect neat organization and unit of command. Business executives have stockholders and government and customers to contend with—public libraries have trustees, municipal government and users—college libraries have the president of the institution, the faculty, the faculty senate, and students—school libraries have the principal, the superintendent, the board of education, and the electorate—the special librarian functions within a corporate structure. So the apex of the internal pyramid is not really the top of the hierarchy. Some writers have suggested that an inverted pyramid be placed above the chief executive, with the director at the bottom rather than at the top.[4] External relations constitute a chain of control above them with which administrators have to work as surely as they work with the hierarchy of control below them.

As has been stated, the usual discussion of organization starts with an organization chart. This is a kind of skeleton, showing basic shape and structure. But a skeleton does not do work; flesh and muscles and intelligence and a decision to act are needed if anything is to get done.

An alternative approach is to start with workers themselves. What jobs are needed to achieve our purpose? Who do we need to get to fill the jobs? How can the jobs be grouped together to provide a career service? What will motivate the workers to keep on producing? Such questions shift attention from structure to human relations, and open up a fresh world, the world of people and not of charts. With this approach the personnel administrator gets closer to the heart of the matter. The rest of the body, starting with the skeleton, can then be added.

Even though libraries have typically been top-down structures, with a director and a hierarchy, they usually have not been particularly authoritarian agencies. There have of course been martinets and little dictators in the front office, but most library administrators, who themselves were formerly down in the ranks, are not much disposed to pull rank and manage by fiat. They have generally used the hierarchical structure without abusing it. All in all, libraries are pleasant places to work in, without undue pressure.

That is one side of the coin. The other is that libraries have not been particularly stimulating places to work in. They show signs of the tradition of the hierarchy, with responsibility and decision at the top, a level of middle managers who seek to carry out the prescribed policies, and acquiescent workers who do their jobs. Unless administrators give attention to individual staff members, providing them with opportunities to make suggestions and to participate in planning, and opportunity to try new methods and programs, motivation and commitment will not be encouraged. Library staff members are not typically lazy or uncooperative, but like other workers they can readily fall into a passive routine, repeating their duties with no sense of urgency and no inclination to look for improved methods and better service. The test of a library is not the intelligence and responsibility of the director but the motivation and dedication of individual workers all along the line. On this score many libraries would get a passing grade but not high honors. The full human potential in most libraries is still to be released.

The lesson is that the theory and principles of organization are useful where they really apply, but that they need to be properly modified, and even countermanded, in actual practice in order to realize full human capacity. The search is for the foundation of human nature on the job, and once this is understood in any given situation, personnel administrators can have maximum effectiveness.

JOB ANALYSIS AND DESCRIPTION

The logical starting point in organizing staff is to define the tasks that need to be done and the specific jobs required to achieve the tasks. The jobs can then be described, and these descriptions serve as the building blocks of the personnel program.

But in reality the administrator seldom starts with a blank slate in a new library. The agency is already there, with existing jobs and an organizational structure. In this case a first step is to describe the jobs that do exist. This calls for a formal job analysis and job descriptions. The results can be thought of as specifications for the enterprise, the elements of the working staff that runs the operation, as distinct from specifications for resources or services.

Job analysis is the determination of the activities which comprise an existing job and also the skills, knowledge and responsibility required to perform the activities. The record of this analysis results in a job description (what is done) and specifications (what is required to do it).

A thorough job description provides information about the following points:

> *Job Title* (as descriptive as possible—not "clerical" but "circulation desk assistant")
> *Job Duties* (as specific as possible—not just "filing" but "registration file maintenance")
> *Organizational Level* (Departmental location, supervisor of job)
> *Salary* (starting figure and range)
> *Educational Qualifications* (Highest level required, special courses desirable)
> *Experience Level* (Prior experience required or desired)
> *Performance Requirements* (Quantity and Quality levels: judgment required)
> *Promotional Opportunities* (Career possibilities)
> *Probationary Period* (Length, conditions)
> *Disadvantages, Problems* (Hours, pressure, working space?)

Application of this pattern is shown in a sample job description, Figure 1.

CIRCULATION DESK ASSISTANT

Job Function:	Serve users borrowing and returning materials. Maintain record of borrowers.
Job Duties:	Charge and discharge books and other materials. Collect overdue fines. Send notices of items overdue. Register new borrowers. Maintain record of borrowers. Remove expired records.
Organizational Level:	Junior position in the Circulation Department; Assistant Department Head is immediate supervisor.
Salary:	(as per the scale at the time of posting).
Educational Qualifications:	Secondary school graduation.
Experience Level:	Evidence of handling a position in school activities or employment.
Performance Requirement:	Reasonable energy and manual dexterity; basic arithmetic skill; verbal facility.
Promotional Opportunities:	Eligible for senior clerical level after two years; future opportunities for specialized work after training.
Probationary Period:	One year; review after six months.
Special Conditions:	Occasional verbal abuse from users; ability to remain calm.

FIGURE 1
Sample Job Description

How is this information for a job description obtained? By observation of present workers in their positions, by questionnaire to incumbent and supervisor, by interview if necessary, by log kept by incumbent. It is essential that only the inherent tasks of the job be recorded, not the additions or variations worked out by the employee now in the position. Extra time and effort devoted to this initial step will pay off in the end.

Now one knows what the present situation is. But the personnel administrator does not proceed immediately to recruit and hire. The job outlined by the description should be reviewed and judged critically. It should comprise a group of similar or related activities, activities requiring the same background and education. It should not bring together unrelated activities (selection of books and stamping them for identification when they arrive). It should not encompass activities requiring distinctly different levels of education (typing and cataloging). Over the years studies have shown that libraries were prone to combine clerical and professional tasks in one position (the worker selected materials for purchase, made out the order for them, unpacked them when they came, stamped them for identification, cataloged them and placed them on the shelves). When such a mixture is combined in a single job, there is no choice except to recruit and pay for personnel that can handle the more complex and advanced responsibilities, and therefore overpay them for the time they work on the less complex tasks.

While libraries have made progress in separating activities by level, improperly defined jobs still exist. The author sometimes uses a small college library which maintains one service desk. This location handles everything from charging of books to reference inquiries from students and faculty. At least two staff members are stationed at the desk at all times, and sometimes three or four people. Evidently one or two of these are professionals who devote a considerable part of their time to routine tasks. At other times only sub-professionals are stationed there and they try to assist students and faculty. The result is overpayment for some of the work that goes on, and a decidedly uneven level of assistance to users. The two disparate levels should be separated, with circulation and record activity remaining at the present stand-up desk which is designed for that purpose, and a separate reference-information desk established. If there is not enough traffic to keep the professional at the reference desk busy, then that individual can devote free time to scanning selection tools and examining new reference materials.

While a given job should have unity and cohesiveness, it should not be made too narrow and restrictive. A wider scope and flexibility are desirable. Give workers room and variety so they can develop. Too narrow a job can stifle thinking and initiative. The job becomes a job and nothing more.

If you want to get a quick look into the quality of personnel management in a library, ask to see its job descriptions. If such descriptions exist, this is one step forward; it shows that personnel needs have been analyzed and recorded. Then the descriptions can be examined to see whether positions have a logical unity, are clear as to level, and are not too narrow or restrictive.

With a set of job descriptions, the administrator can sit down and analyze the organization of the agency. Shifts in task assignments can be considered. Positions can be compared as to level and salary. The blueprint is on the table.

A set of job descriptions forms the basis of a personnel plan. They will be used in everything from advertising an open position to decisions on promotions, and in the various intervening steps such as selecting new employees, providing them with orientation and training, and evaluation of performance. A career structure grows out of job descriptions and classification. The salary scale adopted also rests on the structure of jobs, and, properly done, results in equal pay for equal work. Finally, job descriptions can be useful in any challenge of discrimination and unfairness, for they constitute an objective record of qualifications needed and tasks to be performed.

POSITION CLASSIFICATION PLAN

Once the individual jobs are analyzed, described and reviewed, they must be fitted into a structure that has distinctions, levels and relationships—that is, into a position classification plan. This is a grouping of positions on the basis of their comparability in terms of work performed, the degree of responsibility and judgment involved, and experience and training requirements imposed by the duties of the position.

In a hospital, for example, the position plan rests on three distinct levels of personnel—physicians and surgeons; semi-professional jobs such as physician's assistants, nurses and laboratory technicians; and an administrative-clerical category. In libraries, usually two areas designate the outline of the position plan: professionals and clerical-technical workers. This usual structure of positions in libraries is familiar—so familiar in fact that the existing structure is taken for granted and assumed to be the only plan that fits the agency.

There are junior clericals: book shelvers, file clerks, typists, desk clerks. They come to the library with the skills needed for the job, such as knowledge of the alphabet, typing ability learned in high school, etc. They need relatively little instruction on the job and can handle their assignments after a brief period of orientation.

Then there are senior clerks performing technical work in the cataloging department or in interlibrary loan or in preservation of materials or in audio-visual work. They have educational preparation ranging from completion of secondary school to college graduation. They learn their advanced library skills on the job over a period of time, usually under the guidance of a professional. Various terms are used for this level—technician, para-professional, sub-professional—usually dropping the title of clerk. Sometimes there are two levels of technicians, making for three levels in the non-professional part of the staff.

For a period, junior college courses were provided for preparing library technicians, but most have now faded

out of the picture. Experience indicated that his intermediate level of staff member was best prepared by training
on the job, thereby producing individuals skilled in the
particular practices of each library. Courses have per-
sisted and expanded for physician assistants and dental
technicians, but not for library assistants, essentially because libraries did not hire those who took the library
courses, did not take advantage of the graduates with
technical training. Moreover, library technicians were not
hired from library to library, so no career sequence existed.

Professional librarians are the distinctive part of the
staff. After all, other organizations have clerks and managers, but as doctors distinguish the hospital and teachers
the school, so the librarian marks the library. Just what is
meant by a professional librarian, and just what education
is necessary for the designation has pretty well been
settled. Usually a year or more of specialized graduate
study is required, and in some states certification in
addition. As we saw in the previous chapter, from time to
time this requirement of graduate study has been challenged, on the grounds that a college graduate with reasonable training on the job can handle professional tasks,
but the challenge has generally been successfully resisted.
Usually two levels of professionals are designated in job
classification plans, a junior and senior level, or Librarian
I and Librarian II. In larger libraries a third level may be
added for specialists. Much of the character and quality of
the agency derives from the professional staff.

Finally there are the managers, very few in numbers in
smaller agencies and growing into larger cadres in libraries with substantial collections. A Director or Head Librarian is listed, perhaps Associate or Assistant Directors for
groups of departments, and department heads. Positions
at these levels are typically filled from the ranks of the
professionals, although non-librarians from outside have
sometimes been appointed in the very large agencies to
bring in an extra measure of leadership or scholarship or
public relations thrust, or some combination of these.

Library administrators rest easy with this structure (but

not with appointments from outside the ranks of librarians), and staff members seem to be satisfied in it, although very few studies have been made to confirm this. Perhaps the adage "if it works, don't fix it" applies here, but it is worth noting certain characteristics of the usual plan that could interfere with personnel administration.

No Entry Point for College Graduates

First, there is no entry point where outstanding and gifted college graduates can join the staff and look forward to advancement and careers without getting additional education. Business and industry recruit very promising young people and hold out career prospects without requiring a period away in graduate study. Does this mean that libraries miss the chance to draw in the very best college graduates? Individuals must first decide to continue their education, and this for a field where salaries are not competitive with many others. Recruits come to the library professional ranks only after clearing an additional hurdle.

Of course, prospective doctors and lawyers also face additional training, but these are among the most financially rewarding of callings. Accountants and engineers and nurses and others do not necessarily face this extra hurdle for they can get basic professional courses in the undergraduate years.

Undergraduate courses were provided in the past for librarians in a variety of institutions, in what were called Type III training programs. For a period the graduates of these programs were accepted as professionals and performed regular duties on the job. The Type III arrangement was phased out in the 1950s and 1960s when the library field sought greater professional recognition. A year of graduate study came to be the standard, culminating first in the BLS degree (Bachelor of Library Science) and then in the Master's degree (usually the MLS). This latter shift and awarding of the Master's degree were also the result of the move for professional status, and not of any formal examination of the content of library study, either by librarians or by the institutions granting the higher degree.

Teachers are in the same situation as librarians, with specific professional courses required for recognition and certification. In this case a full year of additional study is not required, and some teachers qualify on the basis of undergraduate courses. Schools recruit at roughly the same salary level as librarians, but in many jurisdictions offer steady raises up to the $50,000–$60,000 level without qualifying for a promotion. And some schools, seeking to attract the most promising of young people, have experimented with bringing in college graduates who do not have educational courses. The results of this approach are inconclusive, either in terms of quality of teaching or the length of time for which the unorthodox recruits stay in the field.

Back in the 1920s and 1930s, many libraries did recruit at the clerical level and maintained a position classification plan with several promotional levels up to professional positions. This opened a career prospect that was attractive to promising young people who were unable to go on to college. Staff members developed library skills on the job and sometimes in formal training classes maintained by larger libraries. Recruits with no more than high-school graduation in time came to handle cataloging and reference and reader's advisers positions competently. Although they obviously lacked the broad subject background provided by college study, many were motivated by their career advancement to take subject courses at community and other colleges.

The point of this discussion is that there are different patterns of preparation in different professions, and there have been different patterns even within librarianship through the century. Library service has for some years settled on the year of graduate study as the route to professionalism. This has the advantage of considerable prestige and of a long period of preparation. It may have had the disadvantage of sending some promising prospects off into other fields which have less formal demands and greater rewards.

Limited Career Opportunities

A second characteristic of the usual library position classification plan is the low career ceiling for professionals
who do not take on administrative duties. This is not true
for the medical, legal or teaching fields. The physician
continues as a doctor, the lawyer as a lawyer, and the
teacher as a teacher throughout their careers, with salaries
increasing substantially along the way.

The decision of a young person to continue on into
graduate library school is usually not taken in expectation
of or ambition for a management position. The attraction
is to engage in professional service. But on the job, after a
few years in a junior professional position, the most that
staff members can hope for is promotion to a senior
professional position, with a salary at the present time not
beyond the thirty thousands. That is the highest they can
go without shifting from what brought them to the profession in the first place, over to an administrative job. In fact,
most senior professionals already have some management
responsibilities, in supervising technicians and junior
professionals.

This is the plateau that confronts many librarians after a
decade or more on the job. Or it could be characterized as
a ceiling which they hit. The library field is filled with
thousands of professionals who look about for ways to
further their careers but see few openings other than to
shift to administration. This condition should be remembered in personnel administration in libraries; special
attention should be directed to keeping the veterans stim-
ulated and satisfied day-to-day.[5] Attention should also be
paid to adjustment or extension of the usual professional
ladder.

Does this plateau exist because so many librarians are
women, who have relatively few fields to which they can
turn in their thirties and forties? Whatever the reason it
certainly does not enhance recruitment into librarianship.
The library that wants to have an edge in attracting the
most promising of young people would do well to have
three levels for professionals in the position classification

plan, with commensurate salaries, for this provides a library career rather than a library-cum-administrative career.

This, of course, is not to denigrate the individual who develops administrative ambitions along the way, but the three levels on the non-administrative side serve to establish an attractive professional career.

Thus a clear-cut step is available to counteract the negative effects of the prevailing pattern. In libraries of any size there exist a wide range of professional duties, up to some that are most complex and require extensive experience, additional background and advanced judgment. Examples would be developing a local history collection or a specialized business section in a public library, or liaison with faculty in an academic library. A natural for advanced and specialized status would be subject librarians, who would need graduate subject study as well as their professional training. Looking ahead, such advanced rating would also apply to librarians who evaluate the proliferating data bases and guide seekers in their use. High-tech librarians, at the third professional level and with salaries in the $50,000 range, could fill a gap in expertise as the new technology develops, and the impact of libraries in both universities and communities would be enhanced. A few libraries have experimented with this suggested approach, with promising results.[6] This prospect will be developed more fully in the final chapter.

Thus, some jobs exist in libraries that call for a third level of professional service, Librarian III or Library Specialist. Salaries at this level could be in the $50,000 range, comparable to the compensation for department heads and assistant directors in libraries and to full professors in universities. The drain on the salary budget would not be particularly heavy because there would be relatively few such positions at the top of the professional pyramid. There would then exist a three-level prospect, somewhat similar to the assistant professor, associate professor and full professor structure in colleges and universities that has attracted and held on to high-level faculty members.

Personnel administrators and library directors would

be wise to consider adding to the non-administrative professional ladder, both to gain specialist personnel and to boost morale throughout the professional ranks.

Sub-Professional Staff

Turning to non-professional staff, who comprise two-thirds or more of the personnel roster, a parallel need exists for a career structure in the position classification plan. While it is true that some clerks take a library position simply to have a job, and assume that they will try some other field after a period, others hold on to the library employment and also come to seek advancement and a career. And the library comes to depend significantly on such workers.

But there is a sharp distinction in position classification plans between professional jobs on the one hand and clerical and support jobs on the other. A seasoned clerical worker, even one with a relatively broad subject background, cannot aspire to a professional appointment without first completing college and also graduate library study. This was not the case earlier in the century, when high-school graduates took clerical appointments in libraries, moved up the clerical ladder and gained considerable service experience, perhaps took some college courses, and in time were given professional assignments.

A return to this practice is not likely and certainly is not recommended. However, for support staff as for non-administrative professionals, several levels of employment are recommended, so that individuals who make an unusual contribution can move up in rank and salary. Exceptional support staff can be taught to do simple descriptive cataloging, to handle routine reference questions requiring use of only standard resources, to conduct simple searches in automated data bases, and to manage serial publications and pamphlets.

Libraries are labor-intensive. Contrasted with many other business and service enterprises, they maintain an extra measure of records and handle an extra range of materials. As a result, up to three-quarters of their budgets go to salaries. All the more reason to give extra attention to the sizable sub-professional component which gets so much of the work done.

The line between professional and sub-professional jobs can easily become blurred. The cataloger has some typing to be done, no typist is available, so the librarian sits down at the machine. The reference librarian has accumulated a dozen books on the desk in the course of the day, the book shelver does not come in until later, so the librarian spends twenty minutes returning the volumes to the shelves. The line may be crossed the other way. The clerk at the circulation desk may be asked where the magazines are located. Although having been instructed to refer location inquiries to the information desk, the clerk may reply that the magazines are on the second floor in the periodical department.

But the distinction between professional and non-professional helps to define the staff provision and should be maintained as far as practical. The user will come to respond and will thereby gain in quality of service obtained.

Libraries also would be wise to consider assisting very promising support staff members to complete college and graduate study. This could take the form of payment of tuition and of flexible work schedules. The advantage of such a policy is that the library would have a source of professionals who have already proven themselves on the job and in that particular library.

There are variations in career aspirations. Some individuals find a niche and only want to continue in it. But most recruits, professional and non-professional, seek some diversity and some opportunity for promotion. The personnel administrator should think "career" and should take all possible steps to make this a reality for employees. Failure to do this imposes a heavy hand of repression on a library staff.

The whole structure of organization of staff, with clearly-defined jobs and career ladders in the position classification plan, will make for effective service with the human resources available. But beware the strictures of rigid organization, the disrupting of communication, the isolation of the individual worker, the lockstep of the position classification plan.

SALARIES

The Sunday edition of the *New York Times* on November 16, 1992, carried the following advertisement:

> The New York Public Library has an exceptional opportunity for a Librarian to work in our Humanities and Social Sciences/Jewish Division. Will provide research and reference service in person, over the telephone and by mail; will catalog material in Hebrew characters; assist in book selection and supervision of the reading room.
>
> Qualified candidates should have an MLS from an accredited library school and minimum 2 years of relevant professional experience in a large research library or similar institution. Requires substantial knowledge of Jewish history and literature and a thorough knowledge of Hebrew. Working knowledge of Yiddish and one other European language preferred. Must have ability to provide reference and research assistance to the public and good oral/written communication skills. Experience in original cataloging and knowledge of the RLIN Hebrew enhancement preferred.

I conducted a little experiment with this ad. I had two different groups read it, one group made up of six nonlibrarians and the other of five practicing librarians, and asked each to speculate as to what the salary would be for the position. The non-librarians, noting the specialized nature of the job and the language requirements, guessed that the salary would be between $45,000 and $50,000 annually. The librarians, knowing the low compensation levels that prevail in the field, guessed somewhere around $35,000.

The actual salary given in the ad was $28,598, this for a position requiring a Master's degree and two years of experience and calling for advanced professional skills in one of the most expensive cities in the country! New York City pays almost exactly the same amount for a beginning garbage collector.

How does one account for the low salaries in the library field? No doubt this comes back to supply and demand. Trained librarians are available in the labor market, and have been for some time. If a considerable supply of qualified candidates is available, there is little pressure to increase salary levels. Further, a majority of them are women, who usually are paid less than men for comparable work. And no doubt involved is the relatively low prestige that the librarian enjoys in contemporary society. Government officials, as well as members of the general public, do not perceive serious consequences following from the ministrations of librarians and are not disposed to respond favorably to recommendations for increases. Finding materials for clients to cope with personal or business needs or problems is considered significantly less important than serving physical and medical needs.

Is there any objective way to bring library salaries in line with those in other professions? Not really. Theoretically a dollar value could be assigned to all jobs requiring a year of graduate study, then a dollar value to the judgment that must be exercised, then a dollar value to the consequences of mistakes made in professional practice, and then these several values could be added together to get a total figure that locates librarians in comparison with other professionals. But how can the judgment required by an engineer or lawyer be compared with that of a librarian in dollar amounts? The force of supply and demand would break through any such attempts.

Library administrators try consistently to get approval for salary increases, but with indifferent success. State library associations adopt recommended beginning wage levels for professionals which some libraries adopt.

The pressure will have to come from within the library field; it will not come from outside unless there is a severe shortage of candidates. If any considerable number of libraries in a state or region were to stand together for $30,000 as the starting professional salary, there would be pressure for upward movement. This figure could be defended as justified for personnel with a year of graduate education, even if people generally did not have a particularly high opinion of librarians.

On this basis a reasonable salary plan could be built. Assuming three distinct levels in the position classification plan for professionals—librarian, senior librarian and librarian specialist—an attractive salary range would emerge. The first level would be from $30,000 to around $35,000–$36,000, the second level from $38,000 to $42,000, and the specialist level from $45,000 to $50,000. This would open a career sequence attractive to top-level college graduates seeking a service field without necessarily taking on administrative responsibilities. Such a scale would be comparable to that for teachers and also for college faculty at the assistant professor, associate professor and full professor levels. To defend and maintain this higher compensation, libraries would have to be sure that the professional jobs were relatively free of clerical and housekeeping tasks.

The library career plan is tied to promotions from one level to another. This is not true for teachers. While keeping the same assignment of classroom instruction, the teacher moves up the scale with years of experience and additional graduate study. There are advantages in the library plan, in that professionals must prove performance and advanced abilities from time to time in moving up the ladder. In the school plan it is possible for marginal teachers to hang on and advance in salary year by year, way up to the top rung. Of course, it is true that in the library plan two staff members—one exceptional and the other acceptable—can move up the scale together, the two receiving the same compensation, until the time for promotion, when presumably the exceptional individual will be favored.

The proposed salary scale for librarians can be pictured in a salary maturity curve, as in Figure 2. Movement along the curve depends on two promotions along the way.

In round numbers, the scale suggested would result in some $10,000 per year extra for each professional. In most

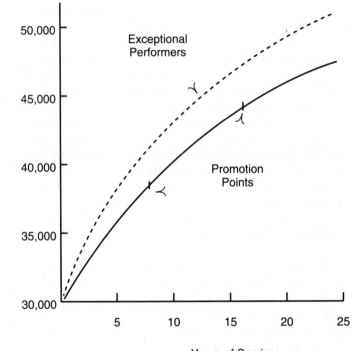

Figure 2
Salary Maturity Curve for Librarians

libraries, with 25–30 per cent of staff at the professional level, this would require about a 10–20 per cent increase in the salary budget, a not inconsiderable figure but still within reason, assuming the 1990s see the economic health that has characterized the American economy in the past.

Different considerations apply to non-professional staff. At this level the library is competing in the local labor market, with salaries determined by what others pay for comparable workers. To get the quality of personnel needed for clerical jobs, and individuals with potential for reaching up to more technical assignments, one cannot start with the minimum wage and compete for the young people taking interim jobs in fast-food restaurants. On the other hand, libraries can hardly compete at the level of executive secretaries in business, or even of waiters and waitresses in higher-priced restaurants. A rule-of-thumb to be considered is approximately twice the minimum wage. This would put libraries a step ahead of bank clerks and department store sales people. In addition, libraries can attract promising non-professionals with the nature of the work and the environment involved, and the prospect of promotion to more technical positions after training on the job. Remembering that 70 to 75 per cent of the typical library staff falls in the non-professional categories, it is hardly necessary to stress how much depends on a strong support staff.

Methods in Business

Business and industry have developed various methods for determining fair wages. One is the ranking method, in which the various jobs are compared with one another and ranked depending on such factors as skill required, mental and physical effort and responsibility involved. The purpose is to work out equal pay for equal work within the company. The ranking is done by supervisors or committees.

With the rankings in hand, similar levels are grouped into classifications, similar to the groupings in a library position classification plan. This avoids trying to assign slightly different wage rates to comparable positions.

A more technical and quantitative approach involves some variation of the point method. Numerical values are assigned to such factors as education or training needed, experience background, physical skill, mental level and judgment, concentration and verbal skill, and totals calculated to differentiate among jobs. Another variation gives dollar values to such factors and comes out with an actual salary figure.

These methods apply more to large fabricating and financial enterprises, with many different jobs for which a fair wage is needed. These methods have seldom been used in libraries, but this in no way relieves library personnel administrators from the aims of the more elaborate approaches—namely, fairness and equal pay for equal work. Nothing can lower morale faster than to have staff conclude that fairness is not stressed or watched in compensation scales.

Merit pay has been proposed for teachers, with those rating higher in effectiveness getting supplementary compensation. This has made only limited headway because it is difficult to establish criteria to determine effectiveness and because of argument about who will apply the criteria. The more typical library plan, with successive grades to be gained by promotion, may in the end be preferable because individuals from time to time must prove their capacity to take on added responsibilities.

Earlier in this volume, where the concept of human relations was developed, the point was made that salary is not the only thing that staff members seek. Such factors as recognition and opportunity to participate and realize self-development figure in the equation. Granting this, dollars are still on the minds of employees. It is notable that when economic recession sets in, workers struggle to keep up the wage scale even if they must give up such benefits as holidays and long vacations. Fall behind seriously in compensation and a library—no matter how compatible and challenging—will not attract well-qualified workers, and will lose those it has.

The plan suggested earlier—with three levels or grades in a professional career track and a salary range, separate from administrative assignments, of $30,000–$50,000—will attract promising young people to the profession and hold them on the job. This of course applies to mid-1990s price levels and would have to be adjusted upward if inflation occurs. Slip below this and seek to recruit senior professionals at $28,598, and sooner or later quality will inevitably suffer.

REFERENCES

1. Max Weber, *The Theory of Social and Economic Organization* (New York: Free Press, 1947).
2. Henri Fayol, *General and Industrial Management* (London: Pitman, 1967).
3. Luther Gulick, *Papers on the Science of Administration* (Dublin: Institute of Public Administration, 1937).
4. Bertram M. Gross, *Organizations and Their Managing* (New York: Free Press, 1964), 223.
5. B.A. DeLon, "Keeping Plateaued Performers Motivated." *Library Administration and Management* 7 (Winter, 1993): 13–16.
6. F. Duda, "Columbia's Two-Track System of Professional Ranks and Position Categories." *College and Research Libraries* 4 (July, 1980): 295–304.

5. RECRUITMENT OF PERSONNEL

Let's start at the beginning, with recruitment and selection of staff. This is the foundation of personnel administration. Select qualified, promising and motivated individuals, and prospects will be favorable no matter what the problems confronting the library; misstep at this early phase, bring in people not right for the enterprise, and services will suffer no matter what the resources of the agency. People are all.

Equally for the person hired, this is a fateful moment. Employees will be giving of their talent and loyalty. Will the relationship be satisfying, stimulating and rewarding to the recruit? Or will this employment be dull, disappointing, even frustrating? A lot is on the line for both sides.

PREPARING FOR RECRUITMENT

Don't jump into this too fast. Several factors should be considered before entering the job market to recruit staff. The job description of the vacant position should be reviewed before seeking a replacement. Has anything changed that calls for adjustment or a new emphasis in what the job is to contribute? Even if no change is called for, the job description should be examined for its clarity and thoroughness, for this is what will guide those who make the selection, and also what will give applicants the best idea of what is in store for them.

Put the job analysis and description on the table ready for reference, and then sit back for a moment to review the situation.

Besides the job description, look at the actual position as it has evolved. If it has been a professional position, does it need to continue at this level, or have various non-professional tasks crept into the job, raising the question of whether it should be classified downward? Libraries have a tendency to perpetuate professional positions once they are established, and can readily end up with more professionals than are needed. Or if the job has been at the clerical level but recently has called for more-and-more searching of data bases, should it be re-classified upward? Changing resources and changing demands can make for alterations in personnel needs. The loss of a staff member provides an opportunity to catch up or adjust.

Indeed, the appearance of a vacancy can even raise a question as to whether the position needs to be filled at all. With the very tight budgets that prevail currently in libraries, some reduction in staff may become necessary; it is interesting to note the planned reduction in personnel in various American industries, making for greater productivity per worker and thus for greater competitiveness in the market. Libraries have not necessarily been the most efficient of agencies and may be able to use attrition as a way to close the budget gap. This is easier to accomplish when a vacancy occurs than via actual discharges of personnel.

In most cases, of course, the situation is fairly straightforward. The library has lost its science librarian or children's librarian or head of circulation and the vacancy must be filled. But don't jump before taking a hard-headed look.

If it is clear that the position must be continued, the next question is whether the vacancy provides an opportunity for desirable reorganization of assignments. Vacancies actually offer a chance for change that may be difficult when staff members are all lined up in established positions.

Before automatically replacing a departed staff member with a new recruit of the same kind and level, it is wise to look a few years ahead in the library's program—or better yet, to consult the long-range plan that should exist for the agency—to see what emerging needs may be. Is there greater need for a person with a different subject background or for an assistant with greater familiarity with computerized data bases or for an individual who can handle Spanish or some other language?

On a wider scale, is the long-range mission of the library likely to change in the next years? Perhaps there is to be greater emphasis on graduate students as the graduate program of the college expands; perhaps the community composition served by a public library is in process of change. Certainly new staff would be sought that is compatible with, even enthusiastic about, what the agency hopes to become in the period ahead.

Will the search be for a person with definite potential, who may become a department head or top-level administrator in the period ahead? The individual added this year may be in the library long after present senior staff members have retired. Put differently, the personnel administrator should be alert to every chance to facilitate needed change.

Other factors should be examined before advertising the vacancy. Is this an opportunity for an internal shift in job assignments, bringing over someone already on the roster who has just the qualities needed? Is it an opportunity for a promotion from within to fill the vacant spot?

PROMOTION FROM WITHIN

Much can be said for promoting from within, for the choice can be made among individuals whose qualities are well known, and present employees welcome the opportunity to move up. On the other hand, primary dependence on promotion from within can perpetuate the status quo when the library should be adjusting for the future. Only judgment on the scene can determine how much to work from within and how much to go outside.

Not just past performance but also potential must be taken into account when considering promotion. It is easy, in libraries as elsewhere, for good, steady staff members to get lost in the group. The very fact that their steady teamwork—handling transactions at the circulation desk without conflict and with accuracy, fitting without protest into the uneven schedule in the reference department—can obscure potential. Take the example of a vacancy as the head of the circulation desk; an individual at the desk who has not thrown her weight around may yet have the requisite management ability. Another pitfall is to assume that an exceptional individual in one division—cataloging, for example—has potential to move up only in that division. The ability to organize work, to instruct others, to plan ahead, and if necessary to discipline subordinates may well serve equally in another section of the enterprise. Senior managers in business and industry often change from one company and one product line to another; top government officers shift from one department to another. The same flexibility should apply all down the line.

Seniority comes into play in deciding on promotions. The staff member who has been in the organization a longer time can be expected to have more relevant experience in just what the library needs and to be in tune with the goals and plans of the agency. But this is not necessarily so. A staff member who has been on board for only a year or two may have quickly come to know the library well and in addition may have special qualities suitable for the higher position. On the other hand, do not automatically discount seniority; the long-term staff member may have fully absorbed the spirit of the library, and may have potentials that have not been capitalized on thus far. It is easy for the long-term staff member to get lost in an agency of some size, sort of absorbed into the regular round of activity, and thus passed over for promotion. The effective personnel administrator makes full use of capacities already within the staff, and by doing so opens up prospects for the total group. Unless some jealousy is involved, one can immediately sense the boost in morale from promotion of a well-qualified member of the staff.

The Peter Principle argues against promotion from within, on the grounds that this removes staff members from jobs they do well and advances them to assignments that they cannot handle effectively[1]. But there is another principle to consider—that hidden qualities exist in the present group that should be brought out by promotion. And this principle has a dividend: its application sends a stimulus throughout the staff.

CHECKING OUT THE MARKET

Finally, the labor market must be scrutinized—in fact, the different labor markets on which the library may draw. For non-professional personnel the market may be local. College and university library directors have learned to turn first to faculty wives; public libraries may solicit suggestions from the more responsible of their present employees. For beginning professional positions the labor market may be state-wide or regional, and for specialists the search may be nation-wide. Each of these markets involves a different strategy in recruitment.

The overall condition of the labor market will affect the approach used. Is it a buyer's or a seller's market? That is, is there a shortage of jobs or a shortage of applicants? By and large the immediate prospect is not for much increase in the number of jobs in libraries. At the same time, there are promising non-professionals who would like to work in libraries and qualified library-school graduates who are looking for positions.

This makes for a market favorable to the hiring library. Candidates can surely be obtained. But this should not result in half-hearted recruitment efforts. Take advantage of the market conditions not so much to make recruiting easier, but to bring in that much stronger a pool of applicants.

A market with many applicants has a negative side. Many prospects will turn up, some with few qualifications for the vacancy in hand. The load of work in handling and sorting out the many records submitted will be increased.

A seller's market creates another pitfall that should be watched. With jobs scarce, over-qualified individuals may apply for any opening and they may be willing to accept a modest salary. But what about six months or a year later? Will the over-qualified individual be frustrated and restless? Try to look ahead in considering any appointment.

GETTING WORD OUT

For both the employer and the prospective employee, the hiring system for libraries is confusing and haphazard. There is no one place for the hiring library to go to put a vacancy into the pipe-line, and equally no one place for the individual seeking a position to determine what is available. Recognizing this, various library groups—the American Library Association, library schools—seek to facilitate communication and contact, but their efforts are not coordinated, nor do they together provide complete coverage. Persons seeking positions in libraries, from their side, try various approaches: answering newspaper ads, watching announcements in professional journals, checking notices at library schools, applying by letter, applying in person, following up a lead from friends, even trying employment agencies.

In an effort to fill the gap, *American Libraries,* the monthly journal of the American Library Association often has sixteen or more pages of job notices, and the weekly *Library Hotline* devotes several pages in each issue to the newest listings. These are logical starting points for professionals. But still the connection may not be made for the employing library.

The problem is to make contact and open communication between a library in one location and a possible staff member in another, with a considerable gap between the two. The object is to cast a wide net, because the prospects are scattered.

One possible tactic is to start "at home" before going out to the wider media. A notice on the bulletin board within the library may produce more results than one might expect. This is a natural for non-professional staff, for present employees may have friends or acquaintances who would be interested. This source may even work for professionals. Librarians on the staff are likely to maintain contact with colleagues, and there may be some among these who seek a change.

Some questions might be raised about suggestions from within the staff, on the grounds that personal favorites rather than qualified candidates will be recommended, and on the grounds that ill feeling results if those proposed are not selected. But there is a reverse side to suggestions from within: present staff members may well recommend individuals who they believe will be compatible with and happy in the organization, and they would not be likely to suggest persons with serious shortcomings because this would reflect on their own reputation within the library. And, of course, any proposals for doubtful and unqualified applicants will be weeded out in the selection process. If this source is used, word should get back to staff members who made suggestions as to whether their candidates were selected or not, and why not.

Bulletin boards might be used outside the library, in city hall, in college offices, even in another library unless this would be interpreted as raiding the other's staff. The word to other staffs can be passed informally, at meetings or other contacts among staff members. It is worth pursuing this lead, because librarians or other staffs may be thinking of a move but are hesitant to take overt action for fear of alienating their present employer.

Local newspaper advertising works for non-professional positions but less well for professional librarians, who seldom follow the want ads. For notices in newspapers and journals, it is worth the extra cost of a reasonably full description of the vacancy. Get in special characteristics of the vacancy to be filled—the chance to work with undergraduates, for example, or with scholars; the challenge of working in lower-education communities, or in a high-income area. Such specifics catch the attention of promising candidates and at the same time weed out individuals not attracted by the conditions advertised. In a sense the personnel administrator is fishing, and the more appealing the bait the better the catch.

However, don't overdo details of the job. One can inadvertently turn away good prospects. For example, the announcement might mention public relations responsibility in the position, even though this occupies only a small proportion of duties. This might discourage some possible applicants who for some reason give a negative interpretation to public relations.

Do not go out of the way to provide unfavorable information about the position—say, the need for weekend or evening hours, or the physical crowding of the building. There should be a fuller description of the job provided to applicants when they apply, and this is an appropriate place to mention possible problem areas. It is not a matter of misrepresenting the job, but of putting all elements in proper context. Advertisements in a national newspaper, say the Sunday edition of the *New York Times,* have achieved indifferent results and are not used as much as in the past. Moreover, at this level, the cost is high in relation to the probable returns.

Employment agencies have usually not been very productive for libraries. The market is not large enough to be profitable for any of the parties, and librarians seeking positions usually use other channels before turning to an agency. But once again the strategy of casting a wide net applies: there is nothing lost in turning to employment agencies, and it is the applicant who usually pays the fee. Besides the private agencies there are the public employment offices, usually operated by the State. While they usually concentrate on manual jobs, this is not exclusively the case. If a library, for example, seeks a beginning-level clerical worker, one with potential but not yet commanding an advanced salary rate, the State agency may well be a productive source. A telephone call is likely to produce several applicants.

The bulletin of the state library association usually gets wide readership, as do any notices from the state library agency. Some state associations maintain bulletin boards and employment desks at annual conventions. Ideally, by the time of an annual convention the word would be around enough that a certain library is seeking professional help, prompting applicants to take advantage of the meeting. In addition, the grapevine at such conventions is active, and the recruiter can tap into it.

Don't forget the library school or schools in your region, both their placement officers and individual faculty members. One would normally turn to the placement office for beginning professionals, but faculty members may be more helpful for advanced positions because they often maintain contact with their most promising students and follow their careers. The library director or personnel officer is advised to maintain continuing relations with the schools, such that only a telephone call is enough to get a positive response. One way to establish such a relationship is to make a bit of an occasion by inviting the faculty to visit your library as a group. There would be a carefully-planned tour, brief presentations by a few staff members and an informal question-and-answer period. Faculties would welcome this opportunity to get out into the field and the foundation for a continuing relationship would be established. The school should have a definite impression that yours is a stimulating library in which to place students and a library that offers future possibilities.

Individual libraries have different reputations within the profession. Some are looked on as progressive and innovative, and others as dull and uninspired. Some have warm relations with employees while others seem to stir up controversy, with word getting around of employee dissatisfaction. Some are thought of as promising places for promotion, either within or in other libraries, while others are seen as dead ends. Much of this derives from leadership of the agency, but whatever the cause it can help or detract from recruitment.

LONG-RANGE RECRUITING

As just described, a special effort is needed to fill specific vacancies, but there is a wider and continuing aspect to recruiting. Libraries send forth an image every day they are open. A combination of the resources they have, the services they provide, the attitude of staff, the utility and attractiveness of furnishings, even the appearance of the building and entranceway, puts out a message. This reaches not only potential users but also serves to attract young people to the profession, or to send them away. Both individual libraries and the profession as a whole would do well to promote the general cause of libraries.

In 1993, the New York Library Association, with a foundation grant, launched a state-wide campaign to "increase public awareness of libraries." The first year was devoted to a public-relations program handled by a professional agency. The second phase moves to local workers—librarians, officials, trustees, friends groups—encouraging and supporting state-wide local efforts with information and sample materials. The emphasis is on rural areas and inner-city areas, where public awareness and response are most needed. While the primary purpose is to stimulate use and support of libraries, no doubt the campaign has also attracted some potential recruits. It is a program that other states might well consider; information can be obtained from the New York Library Association.

Question the residents of a community, the students and faculty of a college, the employees of a business firm, and they usually have an impression, good or bad, of their library. Oddly enough, libraries have seldom gone out of their way to check out this public opinion. Art museums have learned to use opinion surveys to determine where they stand and what adjustments they should make. The museums have learned what the general public thinks of them, what people expect to find inside, how they believe they will be treated, and what those who have made a visit would like to find. With this information the agencies have decided on special exhibits, re-arranged their displays, even changed the descriptions on individual paintings.

Do individual libraries know the opinion of them held by the general public; do they know whether patrons find them easy or hard to use; are they even sure of what hours of service users would prefer? A general public opinion survey, with a reliable scientific sample, might be beyond the financial resources of many libraries, but it is a project in which volunteers could be enlisted. And certainly it would be feasible to question within the building, either by interview or questionnaire. Such market research is not used by libraries; the attitude seems to be: "Here we are—use us if you wish—but don't expect much adjustment just for your convenience."

The image projected by libraries forms the background against which potential recruits decide to respond or not. If not for present users, then for future staff, it pays to reflect on that image.

There is a group that comes to know more than average about the library work and the profession: those who as young people are employed or help in libraries, in high school or college, or when they work part-time while going to school. Here is a possible pool of recruits that is worth cultivating. A fair number of well-established librarians report that they backed into the profession. They originally took a library job not as their life work but simply because the location was convenient or the hours were suitable while they were going to college. Once inside they looked around and recognized a compatible and challenging field of work. Some have ended up as heads of large libraries.

Every library should keep a sharp eye on the promising younger workers associated with it. Encourage them: go out of the way to bring them into staff activities, get their opinions and suggestions, consider adjusting schedules for their educational needs. If a library has a particularly promising prospect, it may even find a source of financial aid to help the individual go to library school. Another option is to offer a full-time position to a college senior who has made a particularly favorable impression, thus providing a source of income while the individual goes on to graduate library study. This would be a kind of internship, with a definite allocation of staff time to introduce the recruit to wider duties.

Why do young people go to library school and enter the profession? What is it that attracts them to the field?

Essentially it is the prospect of engaging in work they want to do. They may be service-minded and want to work with people who are seeking enlightenment and education, or they may want to devote themselves to materials in a subject field, or to work with children, or they may welcome the demands of cataloging and bibliographic work. For people the nature of the work is a strong attraction, and in this they may display mature wisdom. Blessed are the individuals who have jobs they enjoy.

In a sense, recruiting is going on every day, all the time. If this is done well, with consideration for what constituencies and actual users think of the agency, the pool of candidates will not only be larger but also better qualified. The harvest may come later, but it still depends on cultivation all along the way.

CIVIL SERVICE

The existence of a formal "merit system" in governmental jurisdictions poses a special problem in both recruitment and selection. Civil service, of course, came into existence for a worthy purpose: to eliminate personal and political influence in government employment. Over the years some civil service agencies in states, counties and cities have added services to assist their employing departments, thus becoming personnel offices for government. But many of the agencies early set up procedures and tests which they administer without regard to the special needs of different departments, thus creating a separate layer of bureaucracy, and they continue the practice to this day. Should the selection standards and procedures for a police force, for accountants, for janitors and for librarians be the same? Should all candidates be required to take a written test?

Civil service procedures usually depend on examinations to establish eligibility lists. This ties the library to tests compiled by or with the civil service agency. What expertise does such an office have for preparing tests for local history librarians or children's librarians or any other needed personnel? Some attention may be given to educational and other qualifications of applicants, but only if the hiring library succeeds in getting the agency to agree to this for library positions.

Civil service offices like to assign numerical grades to those who pass the tests, then list the successful candidates from top to bottom. Note that to this point no consideration has been given to the individual characteristics of applicants that may suit—or be antithetical—to the hiring library. The agency has performed its legal responsibility of eliminating political considerations in establishing eligibility, but has given little attention to either the particular position being filled or the special qualifications sought in applicants.

Further, the examination may have been not for specific jobs but for classes of positions—Librarian I, Librarian II, etc. After all, the outside agencies can hardly be expected to devise a separate test and go through the routine every time a vacancy occurs.

In the most restrictive jurisdictions, the library is then required to offer the job to the applicant with the highest score, or, if that individual for some reason does not accept the offer, then to the next highest, and so on down the list. In most instances, the hiring unit is given the choice of one of the top three or five persons on the list, but this loosens the strait jacket only a little. The whole system is mechanical and does not discriminate among candidates on the basis of qualifications. It is also slow and costly. Finally, it turns away some promising candidates who do not believe that a written test is the way to judge their abilities as a librarian.

Over the years, as the criticisms of civil service offices have mounted, some agencies have become more flexible and cooperative. In other cases, both at the city and state level, civil service has remained as a rigid system with a noble purpose and outmoded, restrictive procedures.

There is a legal question as to whether public libraries are necessarily subject to local civil service regulations. Organized under state laws, most local library boards have jurisdiction over the hiring and firing of staff. This takes the issue into the quagmire of library-board versus city-authority, which has a long record of adjudication. Most libraries have not elected to bring the issue to court but seek to get along as best they can with the civil service commission.

Library personnel officers in affected jurisdictions have had to learn how to live with their civil service agency—some might say how to get around the agency. Various compromises have been worked out. In some jurisdictions civil service offices have accepted what is almost an oxymoron, the "unassembled" examination—that is, no written test is used but the applications of candidates are reviewed by a committee, as might normally occur outside of civil service. Where the formal test has been retained, the library in some instances prepares the questions to be used. In other localities the hiring library has the right to select anyone on the eligibility list.

It has been a kind of game to play with the rigid central personnel office. Fortunately, more relevant and enlightened procedures have been worked out in many districts across the country.

REFERENCES

1. Laurence J. Peter, *The Peter Principle* (New York: William Morrow, 1969).

6. SELECTION OF PERSONNEL

Judging other people is never easy, whether they be applicants for a position, staff members on the job, or personal associates. In the next chapter we will note the intricacies and problems of evaluating employees already in the organization, whose performance has been visible for a period of time. How much more difficult it is to judge among candidates from outside, where the selectors are working one or more steps away from actual observed performance. Even with all the selection evidence on the table—application, résumé, references, records of interviews, perhaps test results—more than one personnel officer has wished that he/she could simply have the candidates work for six months on the job and then make the choice. But usually there is no alternative to depending on the record and on personal impressions.

Perhaps at no other point does so much ride on a single decision by an administrator. The applicant selected may well be with the library for a period of years, giving outstanding service or marginal service, moving the agency forward or holding it back. Yet this decision will be based on incomplete evidence and impressions. All the more reason to devote time and effort to the endeavor and try to get as complete a record as possible under the circumstances.

STRATEGIES FOR SELECTION

Facing the dilemma of basing a decision on the record rather than on actual performance, what strategy should the selector adopt? First, determine to go through the

95

selection process conscientiously and thoroughly, step by step. Second, remain as detached and objective as possible throughout the process. Third, don't be tempted into a premature or hasty decision. Finally, have a firm probationary program set up, and make use of it, because some mistakes in original selection are bound to occur.

In selecting among applicants, there are two stages or two sides of the coin, one negative and one positive.

Obviously the library seeks staff members with basic human qualities, among which are honesty, reliability, self-discipline, friendliness and productivity. In addition, the library seeks individuals with the specific background and skills required for the job being filled. It is wise to think consciously of both sides of the coin and not get carried away by some one outstanding characteristic of a particular applicant. It is possible to have an individual with a distinctive background in the subject field needed, plus a record of publishing articles in the subject, yet a careful review of the résumé, academic record and references may show a person of uneven accomplishments who has shifted jobs frequently, who works in spurts and is then unproductive, and who may even have some problems of personal adjustment. The decision then is whether the agency wants to take a chance on the applicant in order to acquire the exceptional qualities. Or the uncertain combination may be of an opposite kind, with an individual possessing an open, friendly personality but an academic record that raises questions as to performance.

Negative personal qualities can usually be brought out by careful, even critical, review of the formal record, the job history and the references, supplemented by an interview. The approach at this stage is to ask, "What is wrong with this applicant?" Defects of character and personality usually cannot be completely hidden in the record.

This first and negative step accomplished, the selecting officer or committee can then turn to positive attributes. Now the questions are: "How does this applicant fit the job?" "What will he/she bring to the library?" "How will the institution be strengthened by his or her service?" The record is reviewed not for gaps or lapses but for positive traits and abilities.

This second step comes closer to identifying, among several applicants, the one that should be hired. Most individuals will pass the negative scrutiny; most have adequate personal qualities. Only one or a few will come out on top of the search for special qualities needed by the agency at the time.

While the library certainly wants individuals of good character, productive work habits and friendly demeanor, a word of caution is needed against requiring all staff members to fit into one pattern. Avoid a bland mixture where all workers are "nice" but no one has any particular initiative or creativity. The nature of libraries and library work is such that it is easy to meet routine demands, stay on an even keel, and never reach out to that new program, new clientele, or fresh opportunity.

Equally, the agency will not fare well if all or most staff members are running around starting new programs, tinkering with regular services, seeking to get into the limelight. Perhaps it is good to have members of both persuasions, the traditional and the innovative, hoping that they will balance each other. Better yet, the ideal is to have both qualities in the same staff members, who devote much of their energy to maintaining the foundation of services, but are open and alert to improvement and opportunity.

Procedure in Selection

The steps in the selection process are as follows:

1. Establish the special qualities desired
2. Assemble documentation
3. Do preliminary screening
4. Administer tests (optional)
5. Conduct interviews
6. Do background checks
7. Make the actual selection

Typically the steps occur in this sequence, although variations may occur, when an exceptional candidate turns up, for example, or when a prospect is available for a preliminary interview early in the search, at a professional meeting or a college recruiting office.

Be methodical; go through the sequence. Don't be tempted to short-circuit the process; too much is at stake here. A candidate may seem just right until the final reference is double-checked and a new element enters the picture.

What is proposed here is a kind of hurdle process, from original application to final interview and selection. At each step or hurdle some applicants are rejected. This narrows down the field so that only a few are interviewed, thus saving time while identifying the front runners.

Start out with a general profile in mind. For a desk assistant the broad requirements may be as follows:

> Coordinated manual ability
> Accuracy in alphabetizing and filing
> Memory for details
> Ability to communicate
> Friendly manner
> Concentration amid distraction

For a professional the general profile may be as follows, depending on the position:

> Broad subject background
> Sound discipline in library theory and methods
> High intelligence
> Thorough work habits
> Ability to communicate
> Friendly manner
> Cooperative attitude in staff relations

Then, to the broad menu would be added particular abilities needed in the specific job to be filled, whether typing skill for the clerk or background in computerized information searching for the professional.

The selector is looking for what have been called *can do*

and *will do* qualities. A high-school graduate with a sound record, good service in a preceding job and an open, friendly manner can handle desk routines. The question is whether the individual will actually perform on the job, displaying self-discipline, dedication and effort. Similarly, the library school graduate should be able to handle a reference assignment, but the question remains whether the individual will actually analyze inquiries to determine just what the user seeks, and will follow up to be sure that adequate resources are obtained. The "can do" qualities are easier to ascertain because the record provides evidence; the "will do" qualities are more elusive to determine before the applicant is on the job.

SPECIAL QUALITIES SOUGHT

Sometimes the library simply seeks a promising individual in a general category, say charging desk assistant or general professional librarian. More often a particular kind of person is desired, and it is wise to identify the particulars. Say the desk assistant is needed to straighten out records that have become disorganized, or to assist in a major inventory project, or the librarian is needed to build up a network of computerized data sources or to go into the inner city. Perhaps the catalog is to be transferred to machine-readable form. The final choice may depend on these special considerations.

Of course the job description is at hand. It can be supplemented for the particular situation or for a new emphasis to which the library is dedicated. The personnel officer, the department head in the section in which the vacancy exists, and the head librarian may all be involved in specifying this special profile.

Should the "particulars" have to do with race, ethnic background, gender or such factors? The legal restraints on hiring based on such considerations and the matter of quotas are treated later. What if it would be better to have an Afro-American individual to handle the program in the inner city? What if it would be better to avoid an African-

American for the desk assistant job because all desk assistants already are black? Does the library seek a native-born French person to handle the French collection in the university? Or should a man be preferred over a woman if the job is in the business section of the library where the majority of users are men? To the extent that such characteristics are relevant to the work to be done, they might be kept in mind in making the selection—but only if they can be justified in terms of the job. It is doubtful whether this line of reasoning could be defended in any of the situations listed above.

No doubt some employers—in libraries as well as elsewhere—have such considerations in mind without ever revealing their actual thoughts. Whatever personal satisfactions they may get from such prejudices it is clear that the library does not gain from them.

ASSEMBLING THE RECORD

So the recruitment effort has brought in a variety of candidates. What come next? Preliminary documentation must be obtained for each of the candidates. The size and complexity of the record may differ depending on the position being filled, with less for clerical assignments and more for specialized jobs; less where decisions are easier and more for the tough calls. But it is better to go the full distance and err on the side of a full record.

The original letter of inquiry from an applicant is an essential part of the record. This may vary from a brief question as to whether there is a vacancy and how to apply for it, to a full-fledged account including a résumé. Both the brief and the complete inquiry are equally acceptable as a starting point; there are circumstances where just the initial question is more sensible than over-doing the matter before knowing whether a position is open and what it entails.

In either case, the first communication from the applicant deserves careful analysis. The individual is alone out there, sizing up the situation. How does the candidate approach the problem?—what judgment is shown?—what individual qualities come through?

Then there is the physical form of the inquiry itself. Does it make a favorable impression as to layout and salutation? Are words well chosen and sentences clear? One hardly needs to mention accurate spelling. Remembering that this was the opening contact made by the applicant, does the letter show good sense as to what is requested? Does it suggest that the individual was reasonably informed about the situation and that he or she might be a likely candidate?

Be skeptical of the inquiry that simply asks whether any positions are open. There is an opportunity here at the outset to do some screening, putting aside inquiries that are completely off the mark and giving them a routine but polite response that discourages any further exchange.

Some libraries require a standard résumé, while others prefer to use a rather extensive application form. The advantage of the latter is that it specifies all the information the library seeks at this stage, and the information is in a familiar form and arranged the same for each applicant. A stronger case can be made for depending on a résumé prepared by the applicant. It is a test of how individuals organize their own record. It provides applicants with an opportunity to bring out training or experience which they consider particularly relevant to the vacancy. Gaps which the applicant leaves in the résumé can be indicative of some problem, and should be checked on later.

Go through the résumé more than once. Clear and business-like, or splashy and hyped up—even printed and on colored paper? Any gaps? Does the applicant remember to include extra-curricular activities in school, or community projects, or professional committees? Is career objective indicated in any way? Does the applicant indicate what special qualities he/she will bring to the library? Do you get not just isolated facts but a sense of the personality of the applicant?

Photographs should not be requested—in fact this practice is illegal in many jurisdictions. They could be used to eliminate some individuals because of race or ethnic background. Promising applicants will in any case be interviewed later, when appearance can be noted, so there is no need for a photograph.

The applicant may include letters of reference or list individuals who can be contacted. In either case, references are the least reliable evidence in the record. Surely applicants will not suggest contacts who would question their character, and surely they will list employers who they believe will give a favorable account. This is particularly true if a reference is in written form. A favorable report may even be prompted by the desire of the present employer to get rid of the applicant. In any case, those who supply the references know that letters of reference are legally accessible, which places restrictions on what they will put into the record.

Better is it to contact the references by telephone, or better yet, speak to them personally if they are available at meetings.

Watch for what at first glance may seem to be a favorable reference but which raises doubts when scrutinized more closely. "So-and-so was a satisfactory employee." Satisfactory for what? Perhaps he or she simply turned up for work on most days. Why a weak word like "satisfactory" when so many others are available? If it is worth following up, a telephone call may elicit more insight, and a key question can be used: "Would you re-employ this individual?"

One can go beyond the listed names and call the guidance office if a high-school graduate is being considered, or a faculty member for a library-school graduate. Even then be alert to omissions in the evaluation and to lukewarm comments; persons giving references may lean over backwards even in verbal comment because the remarks may get back to job seekers and prompt legal or other action on their part. If you want to get an evaluation from the present employer of an applicant, it is best to first ask permission of the individual, because there is no point in disturbing existing employment relations.

The author was a library-school faculty member for twenty years, yet received only three or four direct inquiries per year from employers. The library-school instructor may be the best single source of evaluation of a young professional, having had the individual in class and probably having subsequent contact. If the inquiry is made by telephone, note whether the faculty member immediately recognizes the applicant, suggesting an outstanding individual, or whether it is necessary to consult the record. The comments obtained in this way are based on performance, albeit in a classroom setting. At the professional level, this is a well-informed and relatively reliable source.

Ironically, even the occasional unfavorable reference must also be discounted to some degree. If candidates believe they have given references that will support them, and if critical comments then come back, special circumstances must apply. Perhaps the reference—unbeknown to the candidate—has a personal grudge and takes this opportunity to strike back. Or the respondent may be a super-critical individual who seldom comes upon people he/she can recommend. The negative response should be checked further by raising questions with other references.

It is definitely worthwhile to go out of the way to get transcripts of courses and grades for high-school graduates under consideration, and the college and library-school record for graduate librarians. While grade level is by no means the sole criterion, and while special factors may inhibit academic performance, the years in school represent a task which the applicant undertook and the record shows how well the task was done. The transcript is one of the more solid pieces of evidence in the file. If for some reason it is suspected that the college and graduate record does not accurately reflect the ability of the applicant, the results of the Graduate Record Examination can be requested through the individual and will show innate capacity in the verbal and mathematical spheres.

But here again a word of caution must be added. While grades carry definite weight, like any other single piece of evidence they should not be over-valued. While definitely poor grades may be a reason to pass over an applicant, good grades should not automatically result in selection. It is interesting that graduates with high grades have sometimes not worked out in practice. You are assembling a puzzle, and academic performance, while a distinct part of the pattern, is not the whole picture.

The record to this point provides a basis for preliminary screening. One procedure at this stage is to divide the applicants into two groups, the possibilities and the rejects. The rejects include those who lack the technical qualifications for the job and those who lack the quality desired, the latter referring to level of capacity and performance as shown in the record. No doubt there are occasions when persons have been put prematurely in the group no longer to be considered, but decision-making cannot be postponed indefinitely. The rejects should promptly be sent a letter stating that they have not met the requirements for the job and have been removed from the list of candidates.

The records of the remaining applicants should then be examined carefully and critically—possibly by more than one person—in order to identify the two or three most promising candidates. These will be carried on to interviews and possibly to testing. The other "possibles" will be held in abeyance, to be turned to if interviews and background checking raise questions about the small group that has been chosen to be studied further.

TESTING

The use of formal testing in library employment, and in other fields, is controversial. It is easier to expect more of tests than they can give, easy to have more confidence in them than they deserve. But because at times they may be of help, tests should be given some attention.

In selecting employees, large enterprises use testing because of the limitations of other selection measures and because of the time and cost of sorting among large numbers of candidates. Libraries normally do not have a large number of applicants at any one time, so that other parts of the selection process can be done with some thoroughness. Is a sound college record more relevant than the results of a half-hour general subject test in evaluating candidates for professional positions? Is verified performance in prior positions (professional or pre-professional) involving some degree of complexity or a brief intelligence test more useful in reaching a decision? Surely a library would not be disposed to build a test for professional methods (cataloging, reference, etc.) if a library-school transcript is at hand.

Where then might tests be used in library employment? Perhaps in lower-level jobs where applicants are likely to have very limited prior experience, and in advanced positions where some special trait or skill is desired. Tests may have a negative value in identifying applicants who are totally unqualified and can safely be dropped from consideration. For example, individuals who do very poorly on a general intelligence test or a check on general knowledge may be eliminated—but only if considerable intelligence and a subject background are needed in the vacancies to be filled.

An overview of the kinds of tests available will give some idea of the possibilities. It is worth remembering that psychologists and others have devoted time and insight to devising tests and to verifying them for relevance. Those with the name Thurstone attached to them have stood up over a period of time and are still in use.

Intelligence comes first to mind. Most jobs require some degree of mental ability, and verification of this may well be a factor in reaching a decision. An applicant for a full-time clerical position may have only part-time jobs in the record and an average grade level in high school, so that further evidence is sought on level of mental capacity. Such a test as the Thurstone Test of Mental Alertness might be used. This has a section of recognition and matching of words, a section on reading comprehension and a section on quantitative reasoning. Standards are furnished with the test, so that a result above the national average would give assurance on this factor.

For applicants with high-school and college transcripts on a sound grade level (B or above) this step is hardly necessary. They have demonstrated mental ability, and not just on a test but in performance over several years.

Related to intelligence is knowledge. Here again the transcript record is available. For high-school graduates who have gone on to college, or who aspire to do so, the results of a test already administered are also available— the SAT or Secondary Achievement Test, once again with norms for appraising results. And for library-school graduates the record contains transcripts for both college courses and professional courses (the latter reflecting subject background to a considerable degree), and also the results of the Graduate Record Examination. The personnel administrator would naturally depend on these multiple sources rather than administering another test.

The available tests have been criticized as being culturally biased, reflecting material that young people would encounter if they come from homes with a solid educational level. Other applicants, it is claimed, would be discriminated against. A counter consideration here is that libraries typically contain material about the dominant culture, so familiarity with this body of knowledge is all to the good.

Various tests exist for personality. These are designed to determine such characteristics as introversion-extroversion, dominance-submission, self-confidence, sociability, even neurotic tendencies. Here the selector is on shaky ground. These are elusive qualities to try to judge from the paper record and from a brief interview, so the selector may cast about for a test. But this opens up fresh uncertainties.

Most applicants, particularly at the professional level, can "see through" such inventories and can manipulate them, giving approved responses whether they truly reflect the individual or not. Take such items as the following (from actual tests) to which the respondent is to answer "yes" or "no:"

> I daydream at intervals
> I often feel out-of-place in social gatherings
> I like to talk about myself to others
> Circumstances have frustrated my career to this point

Applicants will study each statement for a moment, then attempt to guess what interpretation will be given to either response, and will give the reply which they believe the employer seeks. Then comes another subjective reaction, this one by the test evaluators, who allocate people to different categories depending on their own preconceptions.

Test makers try to counteract these problems by careful attention to value-free wording, by repeating essentially the same item at different places in the test to determine consistency, and by other means.

Also remember the scathing criticism of personality tests in William Whyte's *The Organization Man.* He charges (chap. 15) that employers use the inventories to perpetuate a standard model of worker who conforms to the stereotype of the organization, and to exclude others. He concludes that this results in a common mediocrity that in time is deleterious to the organization.

A library that seeks some guidance on this shaky ground might try an instrument such as the Guilford-Zimmerman Temperament Survey, and then later, in the case of persons hired, check to see whether predictions based on the survey were verified in performance on the job.

Interests and aptitudes can also be tested. For this purpose the Kuder Preference Record comes to mind. But first, libraries had better be sure what interests and aptitudes they seek, and had better avoid adopting some stereotypes. The remarkable thing about libraries is that they contain a wide variety of resources and serve the widest variety of humankind. Seldom are they seeking staff members with a narrow range of interests.

If, in the face of these various objections, libraries still wish to make greater use of tests in the staff selection process, they can obtain samples from the Psychological Corporation and Science Research Associates. Help also is available from standard texts in the field, such as Lee J. Crowbach's *Essentials of Psychological Testing* and Ronna Dillon's *Testing; Theoretical and Applied Perspectives.*

Rorschach Tests (ink blots) have not been widely used in employment testing, although they evidently still have a place in psychological analysis. In any case they require expert help in administration and interpretation.

It would be a boon to personnel administrators if valid tests were available for everything from cooperation to dependability, but this is not the case. From time to time one or another test has become popular, only to fade when results prove suspect. Consider them when the record has gaps and supplementary data are needed, but not often will tests strengthen a staff selection process that is thorough in other respects.

INTERVIEWING

This is the crux of the process. In previous steps questionable applicants have been eliminated—to the point, one hopes, where only two or three promising candidates are to be interviewed. The number should be kept small so that this crucial step can be taken carefully and thoroughly.

In the interview it is hoped that the implications of the paper record (résumé, references, transcripts) will be verified, and beyond that personal qualities of appearance, manner, motivation, personality and cooperativeness will be evaluated. The paper record has indicated that these candidates "can do" the job. The interview is designed to predict what individuals "will do" when brought into the staff.

In many cases the decision on whether or not to hire occurs at the end of the interview, although there may be need for further verification or double-checking of credentials. In any case it is recommended that more than one judgment be brought into the final decision. For professional and senior positions, if a promising applicant lives at a little distance, it is worth paying the cost of transportation to get the benefit of direct contact.

With so much riding on the interview, the full capacity of the personnel officer is called into play. All that is required are the following traits on the part of the interviewer (and this list is probably not complete):

Analytical ability	Listening ability
Objectivity	Graciousness
Empathy	Decisiveness
Patience	Humility

Evidently what is needed is a paragon, an interviewer of endless virtue. Yet all that is available is a personnel administrator with imperfections or a head librarian with a dozen problems on his or her mind.

Large concerns put their interviewers through a period of training—yet even then it is doubtful whether they can instill all the qualities needed. Libraries do not have this luxury so we are down to the limitations of trying to judge complex human beings in the course of 30-minute or 60-minute interviews. If possible, a second interviewer should be brought in, for the stakes are high and two confirming judgments will lend substance to the procedure.

It is useful to have a broad outline of what is to be covered in the interview. Usually the following would apply:

Personal impression—appearance, dress, manner, friendliness, outlook

General background—subject interests, hobbies, other interests

Intellectual qualities—alertness, verbal expression, quickness and thoroughness of response

Accomplishments—special jobs held, projects, achievements mentioned in résumé

Motivation—enthusiasm, drive, initiative

Emotional maturity—self-confidence, stability, positive or
negative attitude
Human relations—naturalness, warmth, tolerance, sense of
humor

The basic objective is to flesh out, humanize, particularize
all that has been learned from the paper record.

This is a tall order. One way to cut the problem down to
size is to differentiate ahead of time what qualifications
are most important for the job. Is thoroughness or friendliness most essential, intelligence or cooperativeness, experience or appearance, dependability or verbal facility? By
posing such questions to one's self and considering the
answers in relation to each vacancy, the interviewer will
have a focus or sense of direction in the discussion, and
will not be tempted into digressions and dead ends.

Make adequate advanced preparation for the interview.
Schedule it, and keep to the schedule. Have a quiet,
separate location, a place that will be free of interruptions.
Don't ask for information already in the record; review it
ahead of time and go on from there.

The interview should be a conversation, with the applicant doing most of the talking, and not a cross-
examination. If this is to be the case, the interviewer must
learn to listen, really listen.

There is some evidence that highly intelligent individuals have to be particularly careful to guard against bias
affecting their judgment in an interview they are conducting. This is not because high-IQ persons have more prejudices than average, but because they typically make decisions very quickly. Observant and analytical, they assume
that they recognize the problem and see the solution
before the full situation has been revealed, and they could
reach the wrong decision.

Every effort should be made to put the candidate at ease
at the outset. Express gratitude for the chance of the
interview. Start with an innocuous topic, such as an
interest the applicant has cited in the résumé. A minute or
two devoted to sports or opera or handicrafts will not be
wasted.

First impressions are important. We all react instinctively to the appearance, manner of dress, attitude of people we meet. But a firm word of warning must be sounded to the interviewer. Do not get carried away, in either direction. So the candidate has long earrings and scarlet finger nails. What do you conclude from this—that you have a vulgar individual with poor taste? Then the "halo" effect settles in, with this first impression influencing and coloring further judgments. The halo slips down and becomes a noose. First, consider whether the paper record pointed toward a bizarre person. Presumably not, or the individual would not have been invited to an interview. You can think of very good present staff members who are flashy dressers, and others who are dowdy and old-fashioned. Was tasteful dress high on your criteria for the position? Perhaps the candidate wanted to make an impression and did not make a wise decision as to suitable dress. Hold off on judgment. Don't necessarily look for people like yourself.

Some interviewers let themselves fall into the trap of looking for one or another key indicator at the outset. I remember a position I was seeking in the corporate world. I was warned to exert a very firm handshake all along the line. I got the job but I am not sure how many hands I crushed in the process. This was also a company where a senior officer put great faith in handwriting analysis; this is not recommended here.

Pick up on gaps or contradictions in the paper record—a high score on tests but relatively low grades; frequent job changes; gaps in the employment record. Probing is in order: duties in the previous job, opinion of library school and the university library, even opinion about the library being applied to, if the applicant has any contact with it. "Why" questions can carry the conversation forward— why that college or library school? Why history or business or literature as a major interest? Why interested in a change of job?

It is appropriate to ask what the applicant thinks he or she will bring to the library and the job. Beyond an assertion of competence, note whether the response includes commitment and dedication. Libraries bring out a sense of consecration in some people; is it evident in this candidate? Any staff is strengthened by individuals who believe that their jobs are important and meaningful.

Seek to draw out the applicant when a particular topic or question strikes a chord; let the respondent go on for a period. Don't cut off comments too quickly out of a desire to follow an outline too exactly, because sometimes even rambling comments by the applicant bring out interests and values, and even limitations. Letting the candidate go on for a period will also show whether the individual knows when to stop talking, which is a virtue in itself. Talkativeness is seldom a quality sought in new employees.

Some qualities sought are elusive and particularly difficult to determine. How well will the individual fit into the present staff? Is this a team worker? The loner or worker who seeks a separate assignment away from others can sometimes be detected in the record or in response to a question about what kind of job the applicant seeks. Another quality difficult to predict is capacity to grow, to take on greater responsibility over time. Potential can be determined within limits by noting the combination of ambition, intelligence and commitment exhibited by the individual.

Avoid leading questions, such as "How well do you get along with your supervisor on your present job?" Most applicants would have sense enough to refrain from criticizing their present superior. Don't raise personal questions, about childhood and family and friends. Let applicants comment on such matters if they are so disposed.

For professional and advanced positions, some interviewers pose a problem for the applicant to analyze. The problem might be one actually confronting the library, such as "We are running out of space for books—how can we deal with this short of constructing an addition to the building?" Or, "Homeless people are coming into the library and using up space—how should this be handled?" A variation is to ask promising candidates to prepare a brief essay on an assigned topic, such as how often to replace encyclopedias or how to deal with pornographic books. Occasionally libraries go a step further and ask applicants to give a brief presentation on an assigned topic to a staff group. If there is time and if the post to be filled is critical enough, such devices can be considered.

But once again a word of caution must be registered. Too much weight can be given to a question or project that may have limited relevance. The author recalls being interviewed early in his career by the renowned Joseph Wheeler of the Enoch Pratt Free Library, this for a department headship. Mr. Wheeler asked what I considered to be the best books on European history. I could see that my weak answer was not making a positive impression. This is a job that I did not get.

Opinions differ on taking notes during the interview. Some authorities advise against it on the grounds that it makes the conversation stiff and formal. Others go part way and suggest occasional notes along the way, but applicants, seeing this, may get the wrong idea about what qualifications are most significant. The author has found it possible to take notes at intervals, keeping them very brief, without disrupting the flow of the exchange. In any case, a summary of conclusions and recommendations should be set down as soon as the interview is ended.

Some employers, conscious of how interviews can get off track and of how interviews can reach biased conclusions, like, if possible, to have more than one session handled by different staff members. If the head librarian or a personnel officer has conducted the main interview, a promising candidate might then be passed on to the department head or supervisor under whom the applicant would work. Sometimes more than one interview can be fitted in along the way; perhaps first if a recruiter has gone out to a college or a meeting and made contacts, and then more formally when the applicant visits the library. If two interviewers come to different conclusions on a given candidate, the differences can sometimes be worked out in discussion between the two, or if the library is particularly interested in a candidate, a third interview may be arranged. Group interviews have been used, three or four staff members talking with an applicant, but this often leads to a mixture of opinions that do not help much in making a decision. Whatever the circumstances, time should be found to do a thorough job of interviewing promising candidates who have first passed the paper review, because the person-to-person exchange is a critical step.

But there is no getting away from the fact that interviews, at best, have shortcomings. How in the world can one be sure in judging such qualities as dependability, perseverance and ability to work under pressure. Indeed, how can the selector even predict a "hard worker?" The answer is in critical review of the whole record, the sharpest and most objective judgment that can be mustered, and having the safety catch of a probationary period.

DOUBLE-CHECKING

The record is now in hand. There is the original inquiry, the résumé, the transcripts, the references and the results of the interview. In most cases the time has come for decision.

But put on your critical cap for a moment. Are there any lingering questions or doubts about the record of the applicant who is being considered for appointment? Sometimes a double-check even this late in the game will clear up the issue. If government officers had checked before making the plunge, say for nomination of some cabinet officer, they could have avoided embarrassment.

Were the references verified in any way, or were they accepted at face value? What of the very lukewarm references? You are about to add a new member to the staff. If might be worth the time for a final telephone call or two.

Were any gaps in the employment record fully explained? Are you satisfied with the falling off in grade level in the last year of high school (for a clerical candidate) or the undistinguished grades in library school (for a professional candidate)? Check back with the school counseling office or with a faculty member. The candidate claimed to have held office in a professional committee—was this verified? The candidate published an article in a general or professional journal—was this read? The references consistently refer to an outgoing, friendly personality, but the applicant seemed constrained and almost distant in the interview. Has the individual run into some personal or financial problem that could affect performance on the job? Here the best approach might be to go back to the candidate, state the concern directly, and then judge the response. A further option is to ask for a physical examination before making a job offer.

Some of this may sound excessive and unnecessary. But there are instances of individuals claiming degrees which they actually do not possess or of taking courses that are not on record. You are simply being cautious, to protect the library, and even to protect the applicant.

Some employers—seldom in the library field—go even further, checking police records or having a test for drugs. It is not necessary to go this far, but what of a test for HIV? A staff group can be thrown into imbalance if a new member later proves to test positive. Or are you by any chance dealing with an alcoholic? Going back over the record with such questions in mind can point in one direction or another.

But enough of hand-wringing. The time has come to make a decision. Who will do this? In a smaller library the director is no doubt involved, or a personnel officer in a larger agency.

Much can be said for bringing the staff into the final decision. This may be done informally, by discussion with one or a few members who had some contact with the candidate along the way. In academic institutions a more formal procedure is often followed in the subject departments and professional schools, with faculty members jointly reaching a decision on a new colleague. This could be extended to college and university libraries, and perhaps to others. In any case, more than one head is desirable in reaching this critical decision.

FULL COMMUNICATION

Full and open communication between parties is a desirable criterion throughout personnel administration, and it applies equally in the recruitment and selection process. Employers naturally expect applicants to proceed sensibly and thoroughly through the selection process—or they are likely to drop the individual from further consideration. Communication also works the other way. Applicants have the right to know where they stand at the various stages of the selection process.

Early in the game those seeking positions should be given clear information about vacancies available. The easiest way to accomplish this is to compile a sheet describing the job or jobs available. Duties and responsibilities of the position would be described. The qualifications sought should be set down, and any special skills and abilities required, whether subject- or language- or computer-related. Of course salary and benefits would be covered, including salary range and vacation provisions. Any negative aspects—physical conditions, hours, limitations in resources, etc.—should be described frankly. Something of the goals or mission of the library should be communicated, thus catching the attention of compatible candidates. Provide at least a few words about the community, college, organization or business firm to be served. Just as the selection process seeks to get at interests, aptitudes, ambitions of those being considered, so the process should convey the individuality of the library to the candidates.

This sheet would go to applicants in response to their first inquiry. Some would be attracted by the information, others who clearly do not qualify, or who seek a different kind of position, would be discouraged, thus making for a kind of self-selection or self-rejection.

All along the way candidates should be kept informed of where they stand. Their original inquiry or application should be acknowledged; they should be told when selection is likely to take place; and they should receive prompt and polite notice if they are rejected at some point in the process.

The library is well-advised to set a schedule and timeline for the operation. This will keep the library on track and will let candidates know what to expect. Don't rush the job, but don't let it dawdle along. Another way to put this is to get started promptly on the task and give it adequate time, and once started to proceed expeditiously.

Selection is a two-way street. Applicants will appreciate a library that recognizes them as individuals and will respect an agency that conducts its affairs in business-like fashion.

PROBATIONARY PERIOD

A probationary period should be considered as an extension of the selection process. The account here has stressed the uncertainties in the process, so that the logical conclusion is that mistakes can be made. Probation is the safety catch to prevent permanent or long-term damage to the library.

In a sense, selection is not confirmed until the probationary period is completed successfully. If this attitude is adopted right from the beginning, by both employer and employee, probation can have meaning and substance. If, on the other hand, it is played down by administrators, out of concern for hurting the feelings of new employees and not putting any pressure on them, the significance of probation is diluted. Present staff members note that it is not really enforced, the word quickly gets to the recruit, and it is that much harder to apply and take negative action if necessary.

This means that the existence of a genuine probationary period must be conveyed to the new employee at the time of appointment. This can be done positively: the staff member is told that he or she appears to come up to the standards of the library and that you fully expect that performance will prove satisfactory.

At the same time the new recruit is told that continued employment cannot be confirmed for a year. As with all staff members, the work of the new recruit will be observed and evaluated. Where change or improvement is needed, the individual will be told immediately and directly. At the end of six months there will be a conference and a formal appraisal to that time. Both the personnel officer and department head or supervisor will engage in the meeting. Any shortcomings will be set forth, along with advice for correcting the situation. Employees will know where they stand at this point. Then, at the end of the year, the result of the probationary period will be decided, and in most cases the recent recruit will be confirmed and put over into the regular routine of annual evaluations. At this point salary is moved up one notch, the increment confirming the ongoing relationship that has been achieved.

All this may sound stiff and formal, but assuming the process is explained early on, and assuming relaxed and objective supervision, the library will be protected and the employees will come to understand and appreciate the standards of the library—and may actually develop a sense of pride in the quality of their employer.

The one-year period is recommended, and not anything less. This is long enough to get a sense of dependability and even of potential, yet it is not so long as to be a permanent burden on either side. The preliminary appraisal at the half-way point helps the employee to come up to the mark. Incidentally, for this to work, the library had better be sure just what its standards of performance are. How much absenteeism can be tolerated, short of serious illness or emergency? How much time off the job is permitted when the worker is in the library? What role do complaints play, either from the public or from other staff members? How much work is the cataloger or reference searcher expected to produce in a day or a week? Certainly higher standards should not be imposed on a new recruit than apply to the regular staff—or if this seems desirable, then the regular standards had better be re-examined.

Workers can, of course, let down after a probation period during which they have made an extra effort. This is less likely if the prevailing criteria for performance have been made clear and if these criteria are actually applied across the board. Afterwards, the successful recruit becomes subject to the evaluation process that applies to the full group.

Which brings us to the evaluation of employees on the job.

7. ACCOUNTABILITY AND EVALUATION

Accountability applies at two levels: appraisal of the institution and appraisal of individual staff members. The two are connected. Staff members who earn high evaluations make for a library that is rated high by its community and its users. Conversely, an institution that rates high tends to pull up its workers, who are motivated to maintain the favorable reputation.

Because the two are connected, brief attention will first be given to overall accountability, even though this is not the primary subject of this volume, and then more thorough coverage will be given to evaluation of staff members, which is an intrinsic part of personnel evaluation.

INSTITUTIONAL ACCOUNTABILITY

Several factors mitigate against overall appraisal of libraries. Some of these are built into the institution, being part of the nature of library service, and therefore will be difficult to overcome. Others are the result of attitudes, of staff and public alike, and are thus susceptible to change.

Impersonal Staff-User Relationships

The staff-user relationship in libraries is in most cases impersonal. Only in smaller libraries do staff come to know more than a handful of users and have regular contact with them. The doctor knows whether the patient is cured or dies, the teacher knows whether the students learn or not, the lawyer knows whether the case is won or lost. In each instance the practitioner, observing results, adds to his or her professional experience and judgment, and presumably performs better in the future.

Librarians do not have such feedback. Readers' advisers of earlier decades did get response from patrons through periodic discussion with individuals and through observation of progress made through the reading courses, but this continuing relationship between librarian and client is pretty well a thing of the past.

Librarians as a group proceed primarily on faith—faith that their ministrations result in education and understanding and appreciation—and it is only because the general public shares this faith in the book that the agency gains support. We are shocked when a school library or a branch public library is closed, but we cannot bring forward any evidence to demonstrate what this does to the school or community.

User Reactions

Further, users from their side are prone to accept service that is less than thorough and complete. After all, the library is in a sense "free" to them, whether in the community, the school or the college; the user does not pay directly to draw on the facility. It is an extra service, over and above the normal activity of government and over and above the instructional program in the academic setting. Practically all librarians seek to help when the patron asks for assistance. How can one be critical of such an open, free and helpful agency?

Finally, the user does not have a standard or criteria by which to judge the institution; no other experience that can be used for comparison. Members of the public have at least some idea of what they want the schools to accomplish, and look for results, but the library is seldom subject to such review.

All this leads to hesitation on the part of the public to judge or criticize the library, at least not openly or visibly. Some librarians might challenge this statement by citing individual users who complain about not finding materials they seek or not getting the information they need. But such incidents are infrequent and are readily ascribed to a disaffected minority that criticizes any service they receive. Actually these expressed and visible complaints may be just the tip of the iceberg of concern about service.

How many libraries regularly survey their users to determine degree of satisfaction? How often do they check after a basic change in the service pattern, say a computerized catalog in place of the older card catalog, or compact storage of periodicals in place of bound volumes of originals? How often do they even have a staff session devoted to possible shortcomings in performance?

Another way of putting this is to say that there is little accounting for the performance of libraries. The agency tries to meet users' needs. To what extent does it succeed? Do we know how many people are frustrated in their search and leave disappointed? Restaurants often have a little card on which the customer can register reaction to food and service, but where is its counterpart in libraries?

An instructive exercise for librarians is to raise the question of the library's performance in a social group of friends and acquaintances. After the first polite comments, if the discussion is open and forthright, the concerns and criticisms expressed can come as a shock. An objective observer would say that libraries lack quality control, a contemporary concern being applied to everything from automobiles to schools.

Staff Viewpoint

Turn the situation around and look at it from the standpoint of the librarian, the individual worker. Most staff members seek to perform, within the limits of their knowledge about the effects of their ministrations. The cataloger seeks to adhere to the cataloging rules without checking on whether these rules are compatible with the needs of the library's clientele. If this clientele includes students just finding their way in the world of knowledge, or if the patrons are from a low-education community, or on the other hand from an advanced group of scientists, do the same cataloging rules fit these and all other possible user groups? The reference librarian directs inquiries to relevant sources without knowing whether the individual has fragmentary or very advanced background on the subject. Both cataloger and reference librarian feel that they are doing their work and spend little time standing off and appraising their own performance; nor is there much pressure on them to do so. Loss of job does not hang over them, and if there is a budget cut and positions are eliminated they know that quality of performance will count less than seniority in determining who will be cut. Most librarians' positions are relatively free of outside pressures in determining their performance, and tangible results are seldom available to bring to bear on appraisal. The librarian shoots an arrow into the air and knows not where it falls.

Getting Reactions

What can be done to introduce some measure of quality control into library performance? Surely we can't cross-examine all users as they leave the agency, but there is no reason why we cannot have them voluntarily fill out appraisal and suggestion cards. Library patrons are likely to appreciate being asked about their experience with the agency, and are likely to give reasonable and balanced responses. Such feedback would still not be easy to relate to individual staff members, except in a relatively small library, but it would indicate what parts of the service program are satisfying the customers and what parts are not. And overall the agency, if not individual staff members, would be held to a measure of accountability.

Surely we cannot stand over each staff member and evaluate every decision made, but we can jointly agree (staff and management together) on reasonable standards of performance. Is it then beyond reason to expect that individual staff members will from time to time appraise their own performance? With a group as motivated as librarians, this might work in many cases, and the results of the self-appraisals would be promising starting points in annual or semi-annual evaluative sessions involving supervisor and worker. Or the supervisor (department head or assistant department head) could work along with the practitioner at intervals, working jointly with agreed-upon criteria and then discussing where they achieved or did not achieve the standards.

Organizational goals and objectives must exist and be clearly formulated if the enterprise is to succeed. Further, the objectives of the whole organization are the touchstone from which individual performance standards are derived. How else can one appraise the work of staff members except as it contributes to the purpose for which the enterprise exists?

Establishing goals and measuring institutional results were covered in Chapter 4. This is the starting point in establishing a staff evaluation program.

EVALUATION OF STAFF MEMBERS

Even if rating of the library itself is most difficult, and is seldom practiced, evaluation of individual staff members must still occur for purposes of maintaining high standards and deciding on promotions and salary adjustments. In a sense this means that evaluation of personnel must proceed in a kind of vacuum. If we don't know whether the enterprise is effective, how can we determine whether employees are effective?

The library personnel evaluator proceeds on the basis of a group of assumptions. It is believed that such-and-such behavior or such-and-such traits will make for effective individual performance. And if this behavior and these traits are present, it is further assumed that the whole service program is hitting the mark.

This conclusion may or may not be justified. If the army is well-drilled and spic-and-span, will it win the war? If the team is enthusiastic and well-practiced, will it win the game? We had better be sure that the criteria we use for evaluation are those that make for the service goals we have in mind.

Purposes of Staff Evaluation

There are several purposes for periodic appraisals of employees, and each is important for the welfare of the enterprise. First and foremost is to guide and assist staff members to develop and achieve full potential. Conversely, systematic appraisal can identify individuals who are not coming up to standard even after counseling over a period, and who therefore must be considered for a change in position or even for dismissal. Another purpose of appraisals is to identify employees qualified for promotion, a kind of stock-taking of human resources. And judgments on performance can be used to determine raises or adjustments in salary.

The first of these purposes should not be forgotten in the pressure to make decisions on salaries and promotions. Most people have the potential for improvement and greater effectiveness in performance. They also need to learn more about the standards, goals and problems of the library they have joined. The exchange between supervisor and subordinate at evaluation time will determine progress on both sides. So the appraisal and the appraisal interview and follow-up should be approached as an opportunity, not as a day of reckoning.

Evaluations which are distinctly negative are the most painful. The supervisor should be sure that the employee knows clearly and fully what is expected, and the supervisor should be sure that full opportunity has been given for improvement. Before steps to dismiss are taken, this is a situation that may well call for group rather than individual judgment, as will be discussed later. But there may be no alternative except to bite the bullet, which will test the supervisor more than the unsatisfactory employee.

Employee appraisal for possible promotion is particularly difficult, because the rater has only past performance on which to proceed. Will the technical skill and dedication and human-relations which the staff member has exhibited in the past be the qualities called for in a different position, say one that requires administrative ability? This type of appraisal will get separate treatment in the following pages.

Finally, evaluation for salary adjustments does not occur that often in libraries of any size, which usually have an established salary scale with in-group steps to apply over periods of time, and with definite adjustments only for promotion to a higher grade. Salary changes are often scheduled and automatic. This may be unfortunate, with employees who are performing at different levels getting the same renumeration and the same routine raises as each year passes. But the alternative of merit pay, with administrators trying to fine-tune compensation on the basis of each individual's contribution, can lead to very subjective judgments and to a feeling of lack of fairness among individuals who have been passed over. Most supervisors would like to avoid this kind of delicate manipulation. But if a library seeks to get out of the lockstep of an established and detailed salary plan, a sound evaluation program can help in making the transition.

Employee evaluation should be in plain view on the table, open and above board. There is no need to stress the appraisal program and build it up into an issue, but it should be mentioned right from the beginning, perhaps under some such title as the Career and Development Plan. Its positive value, for both the employee and the organization, should be noted. For the new employee, formal evaluation will occur after six months and again after one year, at the end of the probationary period. For other employees the review will occur annually. Given this approach, as a regular and positive program, at least some of the tension should be removed. It would be unrealistic to assume that all concern on the part of staff members will disappear. But if the process is faced squarely, and if the evaluations hold to the purpose of improvement and development, the attitude on both sides will be relaxed rather than apprehensive. Of course this starts with a positive attitude on the part of supervisors doing the rating, which itself—as we shall see—takes some achieving.

METHODS OF APPRAISAL

Evaluation or rating implies some measures or standards against which appraisal is done. What are the standards that should apply in library work? What is it that we are looking for?

Three more-or-less distinct approaches can be noted:

Appraisal by traits
Appraisal by behavior
Appraisal by outcomes

These different bases of judgment can be seen more clearly by noting how they apply to teachers.

Teachers can be evaluated on the basis of various traits assumed to make for effective instruction. These include proper organization of materials, clarity in communication, enthusiasm, interest in students, and standards of discipline. Individuals with these qualities are assumed to be doing a good job.

A second method or level of appraisal is by direct observation of performance. The principal comes into the classroom at the beginning of the period, sits down in an empty seat and observes what goes on during the hour. Later the two have a consultation in which the principal presents criticisms and suggestions.

The third method is based on results or outcomes. How do the students perform on tests of the subject matter? Do they retain what they have learned to be used in a more advanced class? This is the bottom line on which various educational reforms are based.

Appraisal by Traits

Libraries depend on the more standard and traditional method—noting of background and traits, supplemented by casual observation on the job. The supervisor has certain approved traits in mind: reliability, responsibility, cooperativeness, loyalty, friendly relations with colleagues and public, and makes mental or actual notes on such characteristics. These are based on impressions, brief observations, made in the daily round of work.

We all use this rather haphazard approach in reacting to friends, relatives and acquaintances, and the habit readily carries over to the workplace. The report goes in on the employee, for example, as always on time, evidently loyal, usually easy in relations with others, sometimes cooperative but occasionally going off alone on a project that should involve several people. The report misses many relevant characteristics of the individual, and may miss those that are most essential for effective performance.

Over time a variety of forms or rating scales have been devised to give a little more system and objectivity to this approach. In its simplest formulation, the rating scale may simply list the characteristics sought in the particular agency, with boxes to be checked to rate the individual. Figure 3 is an example.

A somewhat more complex formulation lists the characteristics and then provides a scale with brief descriptions of performance on these items. The evaluator checks one of the gradated descriptions. Figure 4 shows one item from such a form, usually described as a Discontinuous Scale.

A variation and refinement of the Discontinuous Scale provides a line along which the employee can be placed. This provides more choice for the supervisor doing the rating, who may judge that the individual is neither "average" nor "mediocre" on a trait, but somewhere between. If a rating form is to be used, the Continuous Rating Scale as exemplified in Figure 5 is to be preferred.

	Excellent	Good	Average	Poor*
Quality of Work				
Quantity of Work				
Work Attitude				
Cooperation				
Initiative				
Stability				

*Explain each Poor rating.

Figure 3: Simple Rating Form

Job Knowledge

☐	☐	☐	☐	☐
Does not know essentials of job	Satisfactory knowledge of routines	Well informed on all phases	Exceptional understanding of job	Knows job well and proposes better ways of performing

Figure 4: Discontinuous Rating Scale

Attitude

Lacks interest in work; complains	Careless; indifferent to instructions	Accepts instructions; some interest	Enthusiastic about job	Turned to by other employees

Figure 5: Continuous Rating Scale

While standard forms are available, each agency does well to compile its own list of characteristics to be evaluated, those considered most important by the institution. Once traits are decided upon, the descriptions of levels on each can be expressed in terms familiar in the agency. One such form actually in use in a business organization is shown in Figure 6.

Such forms are still widely used in government and business, and there is a tendency to accord them more objectivity than they deserve because they look rather scientific. But essentially they are based on a rather casual noting of traits which may or may not have close relations with the actual results. Note that a worker may be "energetic and happy" and still not deliver a quality product; conversely, another worker may be stubborn and still produce quality results in good quantity. Note also that subjective terms are used—superior, ordinary, unsatisfactory—that have different meanings to different evaluators. Finally, the same form is used for a variety of jobs, even though these may call for different traits and different results. For these reasons supervisors often feel uncomfortable with rating forms and find themselves falling back on a paragraph of description to bring out the individual characteristics of each worker.

Appraisal by Behavior and Outcomes

The second method also involves observation, but stresses behavior—what the employee actually does, as

PERFORMANCE EVALUATION FORM

Name of Employee_____ Department_____
                             Length of Service in Position_____
                             Length of Service with Company_____

I. Consider the employee's ability to learn and use departmental
routines and practices.

Superior	Learns with Ease	Ordinary	Slow to Learn	Dull

II. Consider the *quality* of the employee's workmanship.

Countless Errors	Careless	Mediocre	Good Quality	Highest Quality

III. Consider the *amount of work* the employee accomplishes; the
promptness with which it is completed.

Unusually High Output	Better than Average Output	Average	Limited Output	Unsatisfactory

IV. Consider employee's inclination to cooperate, in manner as well as
act, with fellow workers and/or supervisors.

Stubborn	Difficult to Handle	Not Helpful	Cooperative	Very Cooperative

V. Consider how much time the employee has been off the job due to
illness, absenteeism, tardiness, etc.

Prompt Never Absent	Occasionally Tardy or Absent	Average	Frequently Tardy or Absent	Chronic Tardiness

VI. Consider employee's *attitude* toward the job; pleasant
personality, enjoys the work, high morale.

Energetic and Happy	Industrious	Indifferent	Needs Constant Supervision	Lazy Surly

VII. Would you recommend this employee for promotion:
Yes_____No_____
(Please explain on back).

FIGURE 6

distinct from general traits. Observation, more or less systematic, indicates that the employee is seldom absent and always on time, works steadily, gets along well with a variety of people, looks about and takes hold of other tasks when public demand is low, reports problems encountered on the job. The rater feels confident in compiling a favorable report. We are still not very near the bottom line—just what the worker has produced—but this is better than impressions of standard traits.

Finally, there is rating based on outcomes. For this to work there must be a fairly clear conception of just what the job is designed to produce, what will be contributed to the library if the work is done effectively. Ideally this conception of hoped-for outcomes should be developed by the supervisor and the subordinate together. This can be an educational experience for both parties. The evaluator must clarify in his/her mind just what the job is to produce, and the worker must in substance agree with or even seek to modify the specifications of what is to be accomplished.

Comparison of Methods

The first of these methods—impressions of traits—is the easiest to carry out and the least satisfactory for the rating it produces. In substance it rests on an image of the subject, usually gained from a little distance. This approach is very subject to the "halo effect"; that is, the appraiser sees one or a few traits that he/she considers favorable or unfavorable, and then proceeds to project from this limited base. Let's say the worker seldom smiles, or laughs too loudly, or dresses in overly bright colors, and the rating is lowered. Or the employee is cheerful, willing to take on extra work, works well with others, and the rating is raised across the range of traits. No doubt responsible supervisors try to avoid fastening on lesser qualities, and may give thought to other traits listed on the rating form, but they don't have much to go on and must act on what they observe.

This method is also open to bias on the part of the evaluator, whether sexual or racial or religious. Of course, most responsible supervisors seek to control or avoid such pressures on judgment—to the extent that they are conscious of them. But some prejudices are sub-conscious; certainly they are widespread in the general population, and some no doubt have come in through the library door. In any case, rating by traits does not bring us to the bottom line: just what the worker contributes to the enterprise.

The second method, systematic observation, has possibilities although it still stops short of the final product. The question is how systematic, how thorough. The head of the circulation desk can readily note the attitude of the assistant in dealing with the public, can see how rapidly and efficiently work is done, can check on the accuracy of records kept. In this instance we are coming close to the end product.

But other positions, say that of reference librarian, are not as readily observed. Once again impressions of attitude, industriousness and friendliness can be gained fairly easily. However, quality of the information service actually rendered is more elusive. Library supervisors usually avoid looking over the shoulder of subordinates, but this is one situation in which at least one close observation may be justified, perhaps after the librarian has been on the job for some months. It is not beyond reason that the evaluator could sit with the librarian at the reference desk for a sample period, a few hours on two or three different days. Responses of the staff member to inquiries would be noted, knowledge of resources would come out, thoroughness in guiding the patron could be judged, follow-up noted. There could even be some observation of the response of inquirers, indicating whether they are getting what they seek. Obviously such close observation would be done only at wide intervals, and probably never with seasoned staff members who have passed the test more than once. When used, this approach, like the whole rating system, should be open and above-board, simply a check on what service the library is delivering.

Getting to the Bottom Line

Sometimes it is possible to get directly at end results. In the case of reference service, this would be possible only by questioning inquirers who have been served—which, as described earlier, is not impossible for occasional sample periods. Where larger libraries provide a separate telephone reference service, recordings could be made of questions asked and responses given, and these reviewed later. The work of catalogers can be more readily checked, in that they produce finished catalog entries, which in any case are often inspected before filing.

Finally, there is rating by going directly to what is produced and comparing this with agreed-upon goals for the position. Does the cataloger produce entries that enable users to find what they want? Do the resources provided by the reference librarian lead to understanding of the topic being investigated? Does the data-base searcher on the staff locate all resources on a subject? Do children attending story hour go on to a love of reading? Such questions bring us back to the dilemma posed at the beginning of this chapter. Seldom is it possible to know the effects of library service, seldom are outcomes visible. Granting this problem, the aim of employee evaluation is to come as close as possible to results. Noting of traits and observation of behavior should have this goal in mind.

In some of the less advanced and complex positions, results or outcomes can be examined, and evaluation thereby made more objective. This can be exemplified in the case of a young person hired as a part-time book shelver. At the same time the differences among the three methods can be demonstrated. Let's say the young person proves to be clean–cut in appearance, with no oddities of dress. The individual's manner is agreeable and he/she readily grasps instruction, raising a few reasonable questions along the way. On the basis of traits the individual would get a favorable rating. He/she arrives on time each day, clears the books left on the reading table and gets those returned from circulation, moves promptly to the shelves and disposes of the volumes in good time. Observation confirms the impression gained from noting traits. But in this case there is evidence in results, the books on the shelves, so a further step can be taken. Alerted by the reference librarian that staff have been having trouble in locating individual titles on the shelves, the supervisor makes direct inspection of the shelves. Many books are found out of place; the young person clearly has been casual in re-shelving and has not been checking the filing. This leads to explanation of disappearances for a period after disposing of the books; he/she has been going back into the stacks and reading for a time. In this instance appraisal based on results contradicts appraisal of traits and behavior.

All this does not necessarily lead to dismissal, but it certainly does lead to a conference. Tracing performance through to results provides an opportunity to correct unsatisfactory work and may rebound to the benefit of the employee as well as the library.

If the evaluation is being done for the prospect of promotion, it is a good idea to work out some assignments prior to the evaluation that will test the individual in aspects of the new job. If this is to be an advanced cataloging position involving the handling of manuscripts, the prospect could be exposed to such material to note reactions; or if a position with administrative responsibilities is involved, the individual could be tried out temporarily in such work. This device avoids the trap of giving high marks to a prospect for work in the present position when the future job opening may involve different abilities.

Another variation in performance evaluation is to compare different staff members in the same or similar jobs. This can sometimes further the assessment process because different individuals often provide different profiles. One is stronger in one quality and another in different qualities, so that the rater has a set of internal standards on which to base judgment. Ideally the supervisor would seek by advice and guidance to bring all members up to the highest standard achieved in the group in each trait. Such comparison does not eliminate the shortcomings of noting traits and behavior, but it can lend a measure of objectivity to a process that in any case is difficult and open to subjective impressions.

Still another variation is to bring other staff members into the evaluation of individuals—a kind of peer rating. This is well established in colleges and universities, where the decision on whether to grant a faculty member promotion and tenure is made by the already-tenured faculty. A dean or department head may make the recommendation for promotion, or the individual may be near the end of a term appointment, but the judgment is made by a faculty group. Material about the candidate is assembled, such as a résumé, lesson plans prepared, articles or books published, and ratings of courses by students. Inevitably the faculty members sitting in judgment will add their personal assessments, which may or may not be fair and objective. Certainly there are instances where candidates have been denied tenure because they did not conform to the prevailing model of that institution or because of personal animosities among faculty members. Established groups may resist adding dissimilar individuals to their numbers. But it must be remembered that the evaluation of a staff member is an uncertain process at best, so that any approach that adds to the exercise should not be rejected out of hand.

Evaluation by peer groups has occasionally been extended to promotions in the library staff in some academic institutions. The device is cumbersome and time-consuming, but it might well be considered in other libraries. It probably would apply only to promotion to senior status in the library ranks. Conducted conscientiously, peer judgment can maintain high standards for advanced positions, and the fact that a number of individuals make a joint decision can help to counteract or eliminate personal slants and unusual viewpoints.

Another use of peer input can come when dismissal of an employee is under consideration. A responsible group of staff members who know the individual would be presented with the evidence of the employee's shortcomings, and then group members would be asked if this checks with their observation. The members would also be asked if there are any contradictory and positive considerations that should be taken into account before the decision to dismiss is final. This step provides verification of the decision and also gives staff members a sense of participation in personnel action.

Any and all approaches and devices with relevance should be used in employee evaluation, because it is a crucial activity for the well-being of the enterprise, and it is at best a difficult task for which there are no easy solutions.

Conferences After Evaluation

Completing the appraisal itself is only half the game. The primary purpose of the project is to guide the employee, to bring out the fullest possible contribution. This is done by sitting down with the individual and discussing actions and activities needing improvement.

Both parties are likely to approach such conferences with hesitation, or even apprehension. Some supervisors are sufficiently concerned that they tend to put off the meetings, and may avoid them altogether, thus defeating the whole purpose. Employees on their side may be apprehensive because they are being tested and may be criticized.

Much depends on the atmosphere or environment that prevails in the library, and on the regular relationship between the supervisor and the subordinate. Some library supervisors seek to run a "tight ship," and if this is carried too far it can make for anxiety on the job. Other librarians are casual and let things take care of themselves, which leads to the relaxation of standards and to a lackadaisical attitude in the workplace. In either case the evaluation interview is fraught with problems and pitfalls.

Given the right climate, there need be very little tension in the evaluation conference. The process has been presented to the employee as a Development and Improvement Program, and should be carried out by the evaluator in this spirit. Handled the right way, the meeting could bring the two closer together and build mutual trust. The supervisor could come out with a sense of accomplishment, and the employee could develop a renewed respect for the standards of the agency.

The supervisor should not look on the post-evaluation conference as an opportunity to criticize the employee. On the contrary, the meeting should start with comment on the positive parts of the evaluation. This will help to put the staff member at ease and will help to generate a cordial tone.

If the personnel system has been set up properly—i.e., clear job descriptions, prior agreement between supervisor and subordinate as to what should be accomplished on the job—the conference will go more smoothly. Instead of making comments on traits—say the personality of the individual that might be resented—the discussion is centered on concrete tasks. Measures of output may be in hand, providing firm ground on which to proceed.

As much as possible, the response of the employees should be brought out, and their opinions and suggestions solicited. The desired result is not so much directing the individual on what should be done as it is for him/her to recognize where improvement is possible. The self-motivated worker is the one who is likely to make the greatest change in behavior and the greatest contribution to the library.

Remembering that the real purpose of the evaluation conference is to set goals and standards for greater achievement, a useful device is to ask the employees to set their own goals for the next year. These should be quite concrete and achievable, such as reduction of the backlog in cataloging, or replacing the signage in the building, or revising the registration files. Now the initiative is in the hands of staff members, and this is likely to prompt extra effort on their part. Interestingly enough, workers tend to set their goals higher than the supervisor would suggest, and also they are likely to be harsh in judging their own progress. This kind of self-appraisal and establishing of goals by individuals turns the evaluation process completely around; instead of this being a critical review by the administrator it becomes a joint look forward, a planning session rather than an examination.

Employee Turnover

Turnover rates are relatively low in libraries, a reflection again of the satisfaction that many librarians report in their work, and now unfortunately a reflection of the fact that attractive opportunities infrequently open up in other libraries. More turnover does occur in the clerical-technical staff, as is typical at this level.

If resignations occur regularly over a period of time, or bunch up within a brief period, these are both danger signals. This is comparable to the temperature reading for an individual; if the reading is above normal there could be an infection in the system.

The loss of a satisfactory staff member at any level and at any time is of course a serious matter. It is worthwhile trying to find out why this occurs. A formal exit interview is the means for doing so.

Conducting this interview calls again for finesse on the part of the personnel administrator. Usually the first question would not be why the individual is leaving. It may be well to ask first about what the person liked best about the job, and then to ask for suggestions for improvement. Some such approach may relax the individual a little, so that the conversation will be made up of more than complaints. Of course, the reason for leaving must be brought out and faced squarely.

Resignation of an employee may be due to conditions or problems within the library, or to outside circumstances in the life of the individual. Not much can be done about the latter, although it could be that a change in work schedule or other reasonable adjustment would help.

It may not be easy to find out just what the problem within the library is that prompts the resignation. The individual who has decided to leave may be reluctant to go over the situation again and may want to leave with as little additional stress as possible. On the other hand, the exit interview might provide an aggrieved employee the opportunity to thrash out at anybody and everybody who has crossed his or her path, which is not likely to be very constructive.

But often the departing individual is willing to express concerns and frustrations, which may tell something about conditions and personal conflicts within the agency. The personnel administrator may learn in the process. Certainly, if particular physical conditions or stress points or animosities appear repeatedly, these should be carefully reviewed. A first step would be to check with other staff members to see if they share the same concerns.

The fault could be within the library, and not only with the employee. The exit interview provides not just an appraisal of the departing individual but also an evaluation of the library and its personnel program. The wise administrator is sensitive to negatives as well as positive feedback.

8. SUPERVISORS AND SUPERVISION

This book is aimed at both personnel administrators and supervisors. The distinction between the two is that personnel administrators are staff officers responsible for designing the personnel program (recruiting and selection, orientation, position classification plan, evaluation system, etc.) and for carrying through with parts of the program not handled by supervisors; while the latter are line officers directing the work of staff members on the job. In many libraries one individual handles both roles; perhaps a department or assistant department head, or even the head librarian in small agencies. Only in larger agencies (100 or more staff members) is there likely to be a separate personnel officer and office.

ROLE OF THE SUPERVISOR

The success or effectiveness of a group enterprise depends significantly on the work of the supervisors. There may be strong leadership in the front office. There may be qualified workers at the service desks, but until the supervisory function comes into play goals will not be achieved, whether the making of an automobile, the construction of a building, or the provision of a library program. Supervision encompasses the whole sequence from new recruit to seasoned veteran, including selection, training, counseling, job enrichment, promoting, and disciplining if necessary—all of these in conjunction with general personnel administrators, if such exist.

Supervisors may not be big wheels in the organization but they are vital cogs connecting skill to production, abilities to service.

In libraries this critical task is added to other duties of senior librarians. In small libraries the head librarian is supervisor of whatever staff the agency has, as well as administrator for everything from budgeting to public relations. What a job! In larger enterprises department heads and assistant department heads are more likely to do the actual supervising, once again along with other duties, probably including professional service.

Supervision is added to regular responsibilities. It is seldom a task for which the librarian entered the profession. Further, it is a task for which the librarian has no training. All the more reason, then, for careful attention to any source that can help improve supervisory skills. In many a library general administration may be at a high level, the staff of good quality, the book collection of considerable depth, but day-to-day direction and improvement of staff at a distinctly lower level. If such is the case, a vital link is missing.

TRAITS OF THE SUPERVISOR

Supervisors lead workers. It is therefore logical to think of the qualities of leaders as the traits that should be possessed by supervisors. This is only partially true. Or, to put it differently, supervision of personnel is a particular kind of leadership, not necessarily that of the business or government leader who marks out a new goal and then signals employees or citizens to follow. While there is no formula for such a leader, the qualities usually needed are vision, determination, charisma, even ruthlessness; this would characterize leaders from Napoleon to Hitler.

This is not the leadership needed by a supervisor, and particularly not in a library. Here the desirable qualities are more modest and more human. The vision or goal of the enterprise is usually not set by supervisors but comes down from above, and is not a personal vision. Supervisors do need conviction and dedication to the group goals. They should also possess such mundane but precious traits as common sense, objectivity, emotional maturity, persistence, and a little measure of tolerance. They must have communication skills, including ability to listen, and they must be able to put themselves in the position of the subordinate, so as to judge human reactions to directives, advice and reprimands. The action of the great leader is to get out ahead, march forward and call others to follow, whereas the action of the supervisor is to sit down with a single employee or a group and develop the best method for getting work done.

The supervisor works individually with staff members; the great leader works with the throng and may not know any followers personally. The measure of the great leader is the taking of the mountain-top; the measure of the supervisor is getting production or service done day after day. In the human relations concept of personnel administration, it is the supervisor who takes the goals of the enterprise and interprets them for individual workers so that staff members get a sense of accomplishment in carrying out their jobs.

Supervision is a person-to-person relationship. This does not mean dominance by the "boss" over the subordinate. Relationship in this setting means exchange. The supervisor seeks support and even enthusiasm, and workers from their side seek clarification of what they are to do and why. Out of this comes the cliché of "the team," the group working together for a common goal. Where team spirit is lacking, look first not to the staff member but to the supervisor.

Empathy, Dedication and Fairness

Empathy, then, may be the most important trait of the human-relations supervisor. Empathy according to the dictionary is reaching out and understanding the viewpoint and feelings of the other party, putting one's self at the receiving end of any communication sent out, from praise to criticism. This is not a common characteristic of any of us. The supervisor has to reach out to see the other side; most of us naturally see the world from our own viewpoint, not from that of another person. The supervisor has to make an extra effort to comprehend the reactions of others.

Perhaps the second most important trait of the successful supervisor is conviction about the importance of the library and the particular service being administered. If the person directing operations does not display such dedication and belief, this will soon be apparent to staff members; if the supervisor is just doing a job and going through the motions, without conviction, soon subordinates will develop the same attitude. On the other hand, the supervisor who is dedicated to what the work unit is doing will find that this carries the day when problems arise or when changes about which the workers are skeptical are proposed; if the boss has conviction, subordinates tend to give the new activity or change a try. Such dedication is not something that can be faked or expressed in a pretty speech that only goes skin-deep. If supervisors do not really believe in the activity for which they are responsible, they would be wise to seek a transfer.

High on the list of necessary traits must be fairness, even-handedness in assigning tasks and passing out rewards. The moment a staff member comes to doubt the fairness of the superior is the moment when response will become indifferent and half-hearted. Once again empathy can help here: the ability to see the effect of recommendations, for promotion or salary increase or a choice assignment, from the standpoint of persons who have been passed over.

A trait that is not listed for supervisors is meticulous attention to details; this can lead to constantly watching over the shoulder of workers and checking them at every step, which rarely sits well. The aim is workers who know their tasks (because the supervisor has done a thorough job of training) and who are motivated to perform well (because the supervisor has convinced them of the importance of the work). If these conditions do not hold, constant checking on details will not correct the situation, and will wear down both the supervisor and the staff member.

The person in control should have a gift for organizing work, with attention to work space, layout of work, sequence of operations, and quality control of the result. In fact, part of the job is to check from time to time on the organization of activities to see if improvements can be made or costs saved. Does cataloging go through too many steps, using up time and money? Are work stations at the circulation desk scattered around in many locations, so that staff members must dash around to different spots in order to complete transactions? What of the arrangement of reference books—are more-frequently used titles conveniently at hand? Are there enough computer terminals for the various work stations? Supervisors are not doing the full job if they simply keep operations going along the same old track. In re-designing work, the staff members performing the work should be involved; they may well have excellent suggestions, they can foresee the effects of any change, and they will look with favor on adjustments to which they themselves have contributed.

Retaining Control

All of this does not mean that supervisors just stand aside and watch while subordinates do their thing. In the end they are the persons in control. They define the job to be done and specify how it is to be done, subject to suggestions from below. It is their responsibility to straighten out any individual who gets out of line. If more drastic action is called for it must be initiated from this point. And they are responsible for what is produced in their divisions as to quantity and quality. It is an assignment that calls for a complex balance of management and empathy.

In libraries the combination is helped and facilitated by the fact that a key part of the staff has professional training and strong service motivation, and the rest of the staff, it is hoped, has a belief in what the library is doing. The task of the supervisor is to nurture and release these positive human qualities.

Yes, quality control does apply to libraries and it is another responsibility of supervisors, another that involves delicate relations with staff. In the two related objectives of supervision—productivity and quality—it is the first that is usually emphasized and the second that is neglected. American manufacturing has suffered from lack of concentration on quality control, in everything from automobiles to bandages. In libraries it is particularly difficult to control because of the elusive nature of the "product."

The heart of library service is the interface or point of contact between user and librarian. It is not easy to check on this relationship. One can hardly walk up arbitrarily and listen in on the exchange with the user. But a regular system can be set up in which the supervisor works along with staff members at intervals, with staff members knowing that this will occur and that it is not aimed at them personally but is an established system applying to everybody, a system designed to achieve the greatest possible effectiveness. Of course, workers will be on their best behavior when closely watched but the purpose is not so much to catch serious shortcoming—these come to light without special checking—but to work out improvements together.

A Paragon Needed?

Does all of this suggest that the supervisor must be a paragon, a super person? No doubt many supervisors have felt so at times. But human nature has its positive as well as its negative side. Workers respect supervisors who are dedicated and fair even if all their decisions are not as sensible as they should be. What it comes back to is not so much perfection in the boss as the quality of the relationship between the supervisor and the workers. This enables many libraries to provide good service.

When analyzing the structure and sequence of positions in libraries, this volume criticized the low career ceiling for librarians who do not seek administrative assignments, the "glass ceiling" for professionals. However, there are supervisory jobs that must be filled in libraries. There is no reason why professionals seeking advancement and willing to try directing the work of others should not become supervisors. In the case of libraries this is likely to occupy only part of the work time, the rest being devoted to regular professional duties, so the break is not complete. There are satisfactions in developing and directing a team, and gratifications in enhancing jobs and bringing out the potential in people. Some members of the profession may properly aspire to work that continues the service tasks that brought them to the field and in addition expands that contribution by guiding the service provided by others. As we have seen, the traits required to handle personnel administration are not that exceptional, if certain fundamentals such as empathy, decisiveness and fairness are already in place.

With some in the ranks stepping forward to handle supervision, we are ready to examine additional characteristics of this task.

COMMUNICATION

Libraries cannot function without communication, to, from and between staff members. It is almost like the fuel or energy that keeps a machine running.

At the center of the network is the supervisor. He or she receives word from above, reviews it with other supervisors, passes it on to subordinates, exchanges directives and ideas with staff members and passes suggestions back up to the front office. At times the supervisor feels like a switch-board operator, seeking to maintain contact and get all calls through.

Thus, the first and essential skill of the supervisor is communication. If a diagram were to be made of the work of this officer, it would be made up of myriad lines of contact—verbal, written, even body language—between the person in charge and the workers. In terms of proportion of supervisory time, the percentage devoted to communication is very high. Individuals who do not reach out to others easily, who feel uncomfortable in exchanging views, would do well to develop some other specialty.

A Two-Way Street

Communication should not be thought of as exclusively or even primarily the sending out of orders, advice and control from the center to the staff member. Communication must be two-way to be effective. Staff members should be encouraged to respond, to ask questions, to suggest alternatives. Only by means of an exchange can the supervisor be sure that understanding has occurred, and only by exchange can the person in charge and the person on the line work together toward improvement.

This means that the supervisor must have the capacity to listen. Listening is more than ceasing to talk while the other person speaks. Listening involves the open mind, the belief that something may be learned in the response. We often hear only what we want to hear; the response of voters during a presidential campaign illustrates the point. The dominant and self-centered personality is not the best for supervision. The receptive person, open to the views of others, is better qualified for the job.

Communication is not just up and down, back and forth, between supervisor and subordinate. Exchange that bears on the work being done also occurs between workers, whether in the formal staff meeting or over the water cooler. Human beings love to exchange bits of information, both functional and personal; we must sound like compulsive talkers to the rest of the animal kingdom.

Thus we come to the grapevine, the unofficial channel uniting workers. Some administrators try to stamp out the grapevine on the grounds that it carries mis-information, but they seldom succeed. Other administrators seek to use the grapevine for their own purposes, trying out propositions along the vine to see what the response may be. This is not to be recommended, for while communication along this line is rapid, it can readily become confused and altered as it moves from individual to individual. If other supervisor-worker relations are open and positive, the grapevine is likely to be supportive rather than destructive. If there is need to counteract, the better course is direct and full information from administrator to staff, meeting the rumor head on.

There is a further dimension to communication that affects libraries: the comments of users that may be made to any staff member with whom they come in contact. Not all of this should stop with the individual staff member; some of it should be interjected into the communication labyrinth of the agency. Communication is news, information, suggestion, complaint that comes from any source— the more the merrier, if it is an energy source for the machine.

Mary Follett has pushed the point of open exchange to the stage of what she calls "constructive conflict."[1] Rather than avoiding or suppressing criticism, she advocates encouraging dissension in organizations in order to give adequate attention to unorthodox views. This tactic has to be handled with care, to avoid building up opposition, but it serves to underline the value of keeping channels of communication open.

Channels of Communication

Various means of communication are available to the supervisor. The media extend from written language to verbal exchange to pictorial material (photos, diagrams), even to gestures and to tone of voice.

The written word is the most formal, definite and final. It is also the most easily misunderstood. The notice on the bulletin board, the piece in the company news, the letter in the envelope states the case succinctly and from one side. The recipient reads it, asking what and why. The writer should be sure to anticipate and answer the why question within the message.

The written document comes best either at the beginning or the end of an exchange. At the start it may set forth the proposal or the problem, and at the end—after verbal analysis—it summarizes the conclusion or the action that has been agreed upon. Sometimes the conclusion may be extensive enough that a memorandum of some length or even a manual may be the result. Down in black and white, the conclusions, the policy may be referred to as needed. And of course, if purely factual information is being transmitted—a forthcoming schedule, a new acquisition, a special event soon to occur—written notice is the sensible form.

But beware depending unduly on written missiles. Absolutely clear composition is a gift of very few people. Words convey different meanings to different listeners. Particularly if the communication involves change and adjustment on the part of staff, the recipients are likely to be skeptical, and the written form gives them plenty of opportunity to think up points of disagreement to discuss with their colleagues.

The normal and customary form of exchange between supervisor and staff is direct and verbal. This may occur naturally in the course of the day, or in a scheduled interview or a training session or a staff meeting. In these circumstances, the administrator can sense immediately what the reaction is, and the worker can question or comment to gain understanding. If the reaction is distinctly negative, even after an exchange for clarification, the supervisor may pull back and decide on a different approach.

It is a good idea, early in the employment of a new recruit, to schedule a session that has no other purpose than to show that the administrator is open to ideas and prepared to listen. The employee would not be criticized or cross-examined in this session, but simply asked what his or her reactions to the library are thus far. Suggestions would be encouraged. The result of this early exchange would be to develop mutual respect and open a channel of communication. The policy of the "open door" (availability to staff members) has more meaning if workers know that the atmosphere inside will be receptive if they elect to go through the door.

Another useful tip is to avoid criticizing staff members in public, whether in front of users of the library or other staff members. Public reprimands build up extra resentment. The quiet discussion is more constructive and avoids an exchange in anger on both sides.

Staff Meetings

Some administrators have frequent staff meetings, others have few if any. Avoid going too far in either direction. Without staff meetings an opportunity for group exchange is missed, but getting together too often can reduce the sessions to dull routine. One approach is to schedule staff meetings twice a month but with the provision that sessions will be skipped if there are no current topics for discussion.

Staff meetings should have an agenda, a listing of the matters to be covered, whether problems or opportunities. The topics will usually be determined by the supervisor, but there should be a regular mechanism by which individual staff members can propose items that need examination. The agenda should be distributed ahead of time. This provides opportunity for staff members to think about the items and, if appropriate, to gather information bearing on the issues. It also provides opportunity to ask selected individuals to be prepared to comment on items that are close to their interests.

Staff sessions can deal with contrasting matters. There may be orders or changes originating from above, from central administration or academic policies or actions of the trustees. The question is how these will affect operations and what adjustments have to be made—even the matter of whether any response or protest is in order. Then there are actions which the immediate supervisor has in mind which need clarification and review. There are problems within the unit which have come to the fore and need analysis and decision on what is to be done.

Effective staff meetings need control so they don't turn into talkfests or complaint sessions. The topics for attention should be listed and held to. If staff members propose other topics, a group decision should be made as to whether to take them up immediately or put them on a future agenda. Discussion should be free and open and to an extent informal. The formality of Robert's Rules of Order is not needed.

For each topic there should be a sequence designed to result in decision and action. The problem should be clearly defined at the outset; relative facts should be in hand; individuals who are most directly affected should have their say; others can add their comments. If the supervisor has a proposed solution, it should be put on the table.

Very often following this sequence will lead to a consensus if not to unanimous agreement. The objective is to bring the matter to conclusion. A formal vote is not necessary; general consensus is enough. If there is a split somewhere down the middle, the matter needs further study and an alternative solution. But don't let issues hang in limbo; a decision must be reached even if some individuals do not go along. It is one of the responsibilities of supervisors to move from discussion to action. Attention along the way should be given to priorities—not just a decision to act, but a conclusion on the relative importance of the action, the place it takes in relation to other demands.

After a meeting, if there has not been full agreement, it is politic after a brief period to speak informally to those who were unsure or opposed, to see where they now stand, to see if they are still functioning within the group. But beware of favoring the opposition, in general comments or in assignments; other staff members will quickly note such favoritism and react negatively.

In a staff meeting, along the way the supervisor in charge should at intervals summarize the discussion. "We are agreed that the problem is serious and needs correction." "We now have the facts before us." "There are two promising solutions on the table—let's concentrate on them." This kind of pulling together cuts off further unnecessary talk on aspects already covered and defines the next stage of discussion. Analysis of the transcripts of meetings has shown that this type of summarizing along the way is critical to reaching a conclusion.

Part of discussion leadership involves the dual task of cutting off the loquacious member and encouraging the reticent. The group itself may well help to control talkative individuals, because after a bit of repetitious talk the other members show their disapproval by their expressions, by murmured reactions, or even by interruptions. The chairperson can keep control by cutting in, briefly stating the point the speaker is making and calling on another member of the group. And by not recognizing the loquacious person when his/her hand goes up again. As to the silent members, they can be drawn in by direct questions or a request for their opinions. There is no point in going too far to get everyone to speak, because some individuals may simply not have anything to contribute to the matter in hand.

Minutes should be kept of staff meetings. The record would show topics discussed and conclusions reached, a confirmation of what the group agreed to do. If some issues were left unresolved, they should be set down to prompt further consideration by staff members and to be sure that they get back on the agenda. The minutes are a record of what the group has agreed upon and of what they will be working on together.

ORIENTATION AND TRAINING

Even as employees have a responsibility to be attentive, productive and constructive in their service to the agency, so supervisors have a responsibility to provide employees with opportunity to develop on the job and improve performance. There is an unwritten compact, each to the other and both in the interest of the library. Thus supervision involves training of staff members to extend their background and skills and enrich their satisfaction in the work.

This does not necessarily mean formal classes, and certainly does not mean lectures at intervals by the supervisor. Informal methods extend all the way from personal counseling to university courses outside the library, from on-the-job training to attendance at professional meetings. The aim is to keep staff active, informed, current and responsive to change.

At times the supervisor may feel like a teacher, a counselor, an academic—and this is all to the good.

Orientation

The first few days on the job are critical for the new recruit. There is uncertainty and a certain amount of tension. The newcomer will be forming first impressions that may well become permanent. The supervisor should step into the breach and build the foundation of a positive relationship.

After the requisite preliminaries—the brief walk around the library, the pointing out of facilities—it is a good idea to start out with a quiet talk in a location away from the bustle of work. A logical starting point is a review of salary schedule and benefits and practical matters of working schedules and attendance. This is a suitable time to be explicit about the conditions of probation. The employee would be given ample opportunity to raise questions leading to a clear understanding of these straight-forward working conditions.

But this would not be primarily an informational session. Here is where the goals and standards of the library would be conveyed. If the agency has a mission statement, all the better. But even if no formal summary exists, the aims of the library and the desired quality of performance should be described. The newcomer should be given a sense of the importance of the enterprise and of the role of each staff member within it, and particularly the contribution of the job now being filled. If the supervisor can communicate his/her own pride and conviction, the task is accomplished.

Following the personal session, the recruit can be given a leisurely tour of the library and an introduction to staff members along the way. Attention should be given to the role and contribution of each department visited. Staff members in the sections should be primed to respond and speak briefly about what the unit does. In each case the supervisor showing the new member around would explain how the job the recruit will be filling connects with the different activities and services.

The new staff member should then be turned over to a regular member of the department in which he/she will be working, not yet for training but still as part of orientation. The relationship shifts from supervisor-to-subordinate to colleague-to-colleague. The recruit may have additional questions and the discussion is now between equals. A gracious touch is for this regular member to invite the newcomer to lunch, with the bill paid by the library.

One more step is desirable in orientation. A second quiet session is needed to introduce the recruit to the "community"—the institution and its program in the case of a school; the curriculum and faculty and student body in the case of a college or university library; and the social makeup and changes in a library serving a city or county. This need not be done by the supervisor; a knowledgeable staff member may enjoy this assignment. There may even be a tour of the institution or city.

Finally, the new staff member should be given an opportunity to spend a little time in any department or unit related to the position being filled. The incoming cataloger would benefit from a half-day observing at the reference desk, the incoming reference librarian in one or more subject departments, the children's librarian in the audio-visual unit. Even the new circulation clerk would learn from a few hours in the acquisition division. A library is made up of interlocking specialties, and workers at any point will perform better if they have a sense of the whole enterprise.

It is not out of order for the supervisor to give a friendly quiz at the end, to see whether the recruit has grasped the situation. Any gaps in orientation can then be filled in. Both sides gain from extra effort given to orientation: the newcomer feels welcome and informed, and the supervisor has a worker who fits in.

Training

The continuing training program is more than a matter of just keeping staff members informed and up-to-date, so they can perform their duties properly. The larger aim is enhancement, enrichment of the job. This benefits the incumbent, who derives satisfaction and motivation from an assignment of more significance, and equally benefits the library in improved quality of service. Enhancement prevents falling back into routine performance, where the job is just a job.

Does the subject librarian reach out to a new theory in the field? Does the children's librarian see opportunity in a new housing project? Does the desk clerk welcome the computerized record? The result of training should be an added component in the work place.

Of course practical, down-to-earth instruction must be given to the new employee. The clerk in the acquisition department must know exactly what records are kept and why they are kept. The acquisition process must be gone through step-by-step. The desk attendant must know the circulation process, the variations among types of materials, and the overdue system. Such practical training may be delegated to an experienced member of the department, and this individual may work along with the recruit for a period.

This is the point at which to get across the standard of performance that is expected. The administrator and the worker may have different perspectives as to approved and disapproved actions. The book shelver caught reading in a corner, after shelving all the returned books, may honestly think that his/her job is done properly; the supervisor sees this as an opportunity to check the filing of materials on the shelves. The clerk at the charge-out desk, talking to a friend while continuing to handle transactions, may see nothing wrong in the situation; the standards of the library disagree. Reference librarians spending excessive time in pursuing complex questions that have caught their interest may simply feel that this is giving thorough service. Each worker may feel genuinely misused when reprimanded.

There are lessons in such situations. Orientation and training have not communicated the wider view of the enterprise, the need to catch up on related work during slack periods, the impression created by gossiping staff members, the necessity to allocate time in the interest of overall productivity. A gap remains between supervisor and expected standards. The training program should be re-examined.

Cooperation and coordination are important in training. How does the work of one unit relate to the work of another? There are various connections to be clarified:

> Cataloging in relation to reference
> General reference in relation to subject departments
> Circulation desk and other units with circulating material
> Adult and children's departments
> Acquisition in relation to the various service units

The object is coordinated effort aimed at overall goals.

One method to be used for this purpose is temporary assignment of staff to another unit, an in-house exchange program. Before completing the special assignment, the "outsider" should sit down with the regular staff of the unit and pass on any observations or suggestions that have occurred during the exchange period.

Do professionals need a training period? After all, they have completed a year of graduate study. What is the shelf life of the MLS degree? Hardly more than five or ten years at most. Certainly professionals need an introduction to the individual library, its aims and problems, new programs underway or anticipated. Early on-the-job training should include as much as possible about the clientele, its interests, its demands, its peculiarities. A period should be allowed for the professional to study the collection, seeking out its strengths and weaknesses. Ideally the professional should know both the library and the community after a month on the job.

Enhancement Training

A library, whether in an institution or a community, sits at the nerve center of its environment. Whatever is happening in that environment affects the library, whether in information and materials that should be added to the collection or in requests coming from users. Should the reference librarian sit there uninformed as a new subject major is being instituted in the university? Should the public librarian be indifferent to the new plan of development adopted by the city? Should the cataloger, noting the spread of computerization, continue to force books on computing into an inadequate niche in the Dewey Decimal schedule?

A multiplicity of sources and methods are available to keep the staff informed, alert and responsive. Word can be brought into the library in the form of speakers or video tapes or workshops. Staff can go out—to the faculty meeting, to the town council session, to the labor union, to the theatrical repertory group—to learn what is going on. And they should be expected to do so and given time to do so. If the library is the communication center for ideas and trends and developments, staff members should participate in them.

Particularly does this apply to new forms of computerized information and to evolving electronic communication. Where else would be more directly affected by these developments? Where else could students and residents turn to keep up with the cutting edge?

It is incumbent upon the supervisor to establish and keep open these connections. It is a test of that individual's ingenuity to keep staff in touch with their community and changes in it. In the process the supervisor adds to the substance of staff members' jobs, enhancing both the background and the satisfaction of workers.

For some reason, library staff members do not often take formal courses in nearby colleges and universities, nor do libraries often provide time or tuition for the purpose. This would seem to be a natural, for everything from revisionist views of history to current investments, from child psychology to political changes in Europe. Many librarians work with such fields every day but evidently depend on course work done well in the past for their knowledge of the content of materials acquired or the substance of inquiries from users. In most cases the librarian remains as the keeper of the books rather than a follower of the content contained in those books. The librarian handles the library on the basis of a liberal education gained a generation ago. Lawyers go back to school, as do doctors and teachers and engineers, but not librarians. The closest this profession comes to a program of continuing education is one-week seminars in connection with national library conventions.

Enhance! Enrich! Cultivate! Broaden! Everybody gains. The user gets better service, the staff member has a sense of achievement, the supervisor gains a dividend.

Counseling

One hesitates to place still another responsibility on the shoulders of the supervisor, but inevitably some personal problems and grievances will arise in a work unit. These matters may grow directly out of the workplace and actions taken by the supervisor, or they may derive from problems off the job. In any case the personnel administrator or supervisor must step in and try to correct the situation.

This may not be easy. Human beings are made up of a complex bundle of reactions and emotions. As one hears about each individual case, it stretches credulity that people get so mixed up.

Way back in the Hawthorne experiments of Elton Mayo in the 1920s and 1930s (see chapter 3 on Human Relations) it became clear that many personnel problems could be handled by non-directive interviews. Western Electric and then other companies set up regular counseling services with specially-trained interviewers. Since then separate units have usually been discontinued and the counseling function put upon the line supervisor. The difficulties appear on the job and may grow out of the job, so this proved to be the location to deal with them.

For work grievances, this is the sensible approach. The worker has what he/she considers to be a legitimate gripe. The supervisor can sit down with the individual and discuss the matter. The first rule for the personnel officer is to listen carefully and completely to the complaint. Don't interrupt; get it all out on the table. Then quietly give the administrative view on the matter. If supervision has been fair and even-handed, this will often serve to cool off the complainer. Avoid getting into an argument. If the employee does not accept the explanation, it is a good idea to have a cooling-off period of a day or a week, and then sit down again to see how it looks. At the least, the staff member will feel that the complaint is being taken seriously, and this alone will dampen emotions.

Many problems arise from stress arising from a staff member's personal difficulties outside the library. These could be health matters or family and marital concerns. Here, of course, supervisors have limited ability to help, but even here they can be sympathetic listeners. If the worker has had frequent absences, or appears distraught or antagonistic on the job, it is reasonable for the supervisor to suggest a session to see if the library can be of any help. The simple fact of having a patient listener may ease the tension at least enough to permit performance up to standard.

Cases of severe psychological dysfunction can arise. Supervisors are not able and cannot be expected to function as mental professionals in this event, and it is not wise to try to do so. The most help that can be given is to suggest sources to which the troubled individual can turn.

There is the question of how much tolerance or leeway should be allowed. No one of us is perfect. If a reliable and effective employee missteps very occasionally, it may be possible to live with this without hurting the enterprise. The author recalls a case in point from his own experience.

When I worked in publishing for some years, I had a very able secretary—organized, friendly, thorough. Just about once a month this fine lady would come back from a long lunch clearly under the influence of alcohol. I didn't know whether she had been out with "the girls" or with a boy friend. The odor of martinis was unmistakable, she was excessively friendly, and after a little she would slump down at her desk and look at it as though she had never seen it before. When I saw her arms dangle at her side, I would say to her that she seemed to be tired and should go home for the rest of the day, to which she immediately agreed. The next morning she would be back on the job, completely sober, alert and ready to go. We never discussed these incidents but I am sure she realized that I recognized the situation.

Other administrators may disagree with me, but I was willing to do without my fine secretary a half day each month.

Problem Cases

But there is no point in being sentimental. Every barrel has some bad apples. Some employees look for loopholes.

Is it possible to report sick for a period and still get paid, even though no illness is involved? Is it possible to stay after hours and use library-owned paper to run off hundreds of notices for a personal activity? Are checks and balances so haphazard that some individuals can cut standards? Is threatened punishment postponed so that various employees see they can cut corners with impunity? There is a streak in human nature that looks for the easy way out.

Obviously, if staff members are caught violating standards, and if evidence of the infraction is at hand, disciplinary action should be taken immediately. Depending on the nature of the violation, a reprimand may be in order, with the threat of dismissal if there is repetition. No matter how humane and empathetic administration may be, disciplinary action when called for should be prompt, forthright and decisive. This need not mean a "tight ship" hour-by-hour, but it does mean a ship that has a goal and that will be kept on course.

But often the problem is that infractions occur and there is no clear evidence as to who the culprit may be. The lesson here is that what is expected, the standard to be achieved, should be made crystal clear to all staff, and equally the steps that will be taken if there are violations. The situation can be reported at a staff meeting so that the offender knows that the situation is being watched. In a loyal staff, some individuals may be motivated to identify the person who is out of line. The staff closing ranks may inhibit the individual violating the rules.

Staff members for the most part will respect reasonable standards that are regularly and fairly administered; equally, they will respect prompt action by supervisors. Infractions are deviations from the joint goal and the joint effort; thus there is an inclination for motivated staff to help correct the problem, so that all can get back to the common objective.

It is interesting to note that when problems arise in personnel administration, often there is no one decisive step that will correct the situation; rather, the strength of the total system comes into play and sets things right. If the whole organism is sound, the body can survive setbacks; if personnel administration is sound, deviant behavior can be brought into line and the enterprise will go forward.

QUIZ FOR SUPERVISORS

If the supervisor carries this heavy load, from orientation to enhancement, from training to counseling, it pays for this individual to do a self-appraisal from time to time. Ask yourself the following questions:

1. Do you have a goodly measure of enthusiasm toward your job, your staff, and the community or agency you serve?
2. Is your empathy as strong as it ever was? Do you look at the jobs from the worker's standpoint?
3. Are you sure that all staff members know what you expect from them, in terms of output, quality and attitude?

4. Do you discuss performance with staff members at regular intervals (at least twice a year) and prepare a formal evaluation annually?
5. Within the past year, have you reviewed the arrangement and efficiency of each work location under your jurisdiction?
6. Do you go to bat with the front office when any order or policy unduly affects your workers?
7. Have you carried through a thorough orientation of any new members who have joined your group recently?
8. What of broadening or stimulating experiences for your contingent?
9. Are you sure that you have dealt fairly with each and every individual under your supervision?
10. Do you go out of your way to inform other departments and supervisors of changes and developments in your unit?
11. Do you make a special effort to keep up with professional and technological developments that might affect your library, particularly developments in computerization and communication?
12. Do you believe that you have become more effective in your job as supervisor since you were appointed? If not, why not?

You should be able to answer positively to each of these questions. These are the considerations by which you are judged by both your subordinates and your superiors. Most importantly, they are the traits and actions by which you should judge yourself.

THE EMERGING PROSPECT

We have seen personnel administration move from authoritarian command to constructive leadership in the course of the 20th century. Down at the level of the workplace, the development has been from the supervisor as foreman (tell them what to do and see that they do it) to facilitator (bring out the best in workers to get the job done). Call it the human relations movement.

In the process the role and responsibilities of personnel administrators in general and of supervisors in particular have increased and become more complex. We have seen the job of the supervisor expand to include:

- teacher
- adviser
- innovator
- organizer
- coordinator

Perhaps the best single term is "facilitator." Now we are about to add "promoter of change."

To an extent libraries have reflected this development over the years. They never were as authoritarian as factories and construction jobs, but in the early decades of the century they depended on strong central administration—Dewey, Putnam, Lydenberg, Milam, Metcalf. These and other strong characters moved libraries into the modern era. Today's chief administrators are more multi-dimensional and inconspicuous figures; they keep the institution going under the burden of multiplex resources, expanding demands and limited budgets. As individuals they do not stand out the way their predecessors did.

Within departments, personnel administration is usually amiable and friendly, with elements of human-relations supervision. However, personnel administrators in libraries have not widely accepted the newer methods, such as group planning and decision making, team arrangements with interchangeable jobs, and quality control. Effective supervision depends on the professionalism of part of the staff and on the good will of non-professionals who are attracted to libraries.

This generally beneficial and non-authoritarian nature of personnel administration in libraries has a negative side. Libraries go along from year to year—in fact from generation to generation—without much change. No doubt this can be traced back to the director's office, for these have been the years of stable and steady administration devoted to expansion in collections and staffs. Whether this is what should have occurred is not a matter for analysis in this volume. But equally, the fixed course comes back to librarians on the job who become settled in their ways.

The enterprise in which one works as a staff member becomes an environment. Just as home and family and community provide a familiar environment off the job, so the workplace and working colleagues serve the same purpose on the job, and a person spends close to half his/her waking hours there. Workers function within this environment, taking it on as a kind of protection. Most employees are relaxed and comfortable within this situation, although some may be tense and resentful, but in either case the workplace still serves as their world when they are on the job. Most staff members, consciously or unconsciously, not only accept the work environment but come to cherish it and feel defensive about it. It is what they know, what they come to each day. They would like it to be there and to remain unchanged. They don't want to come to the library and find that somehow its purposes have been changed, its policies altered, its jobs juggled, its personnel shifted. In a sense it is theirs as it stands, and they don't want it tampered with.

Then, into this climate come managers who, for whatever reason, introduce some change in the organization. Their motives may be of the very best and the proposed changes may well improve the agency. Nonetheless the alterations are opposed, not because employees objectively are against progress but because they don't want that familiar work environment modified. They are likely to find that their fellow employees feel the same way, and thus a coalition of opposition comes into existence.

It is hard to say whether library staff groups are more or less likely to resist change than other working groups; probably they are neither better or worse than others. Librarians as trained professionals should be quick to see the advantages of desirable change, but they are also human beings seeking the same group satisfactions as others. Being professionals, they may be more adept at resisting change, for it can violate their training and indoctrination. It would be a mistake to think that workers within a library are entirely flexible and ready to plunge into new ventures. In many respects libraries are traditional institutions, doing today what they have done for some time, with much the same aims and policies, much the same attractions and individualities. The work that staff members do has also been there for a considerable period. It is because of compatibility with this environment that recruits have entered the profession.

So it must be recognized that any plan of change will not only be logically considered by employees but will also have to go through the filter of their attitudes. These attitudes reflect the personal history of the individual and the social environment at work. Cohesive group feelings have been built up, and have as much force as the logic of progress.

Thus the situation becomes more complex. It is not solely a matter of persuasion but also of psychological adjustment.

The result is that neither in the front office nor down on the line are libraries well adapted for change. Library administration keeps the agency going, with some adjustments at the fringes because of computers and centralized data bases. Despite these peripheral adjustments, library policies and methods have remained much the same for several generations. Librarians of fifty years ago could move into most agencies and pick up their duties in a short time, after a brief introduction to a few new indexes. Similarly, users who gained their library skills in the 1940s and 1950s can readily adjust to the libraries of today, after a brief period playing around with the computerized catalog. Libraries for the most part have been steady and stable in a changing world.

The question now is whether this is enough for the period ahead. No doubt, much of needed change and development must come from chief administrators, but it must be carried into practice down at the level of group supervision and the immediate workplace.

What is the prospect ahead? That will be our topic after a summary of legal considerations that bear on personnel administration.

REFERENCES

1. Mary Parker Follett, *Dynamic Administration: The Papers of Mary Parker Follett,* ed. Henry C. Metcalf and L. Urwick (New York: Harper, 1941).

9. LEGAL FACTORS IN PERSONNEL ADMINISTRATION

There is no escaping the law. Over the years various legal requirements have been adopted in the interest of fairness in treatment of personnel in business, industry and government, affecting matters from recruiting to unionization, and covering discrimination and disability and minimum wages and now sexual harassment.

Personnel administrators are not very comfortable with these laws and regulations—in fact, are not very well informed about them. They are looked on as restrictions imposed from the outside. Administrators feel that Big Brother is looking over their shoulders.

Official regulations relating to personnel come from all sides and all levels of government. They come first in the form of federal laws, supplemented by administrative requirements and executive orders to carry out the laws. Then there are court cases interpreting the laws and executive action plus arbitration rulings and labor-relations board decisions. Add to these state statutes and local ordinances, some of which are not necessarily the same as the national provisions (for example, there is a federally mandated minimum rate of pay per hour, but this is exceeded in some jurisdictions by state legislation). Turn around and there is a legal requirement in your path.

Personnel administrators in libraries often share these feelings of restriction and frustration. After all, they are convinced that they carry out their duties fairly, without discrimination or favoritism. Why then should extraneous rules be placed upon them?

LIBRARIES INCLUDED

However, there is no provision in the laws that excludes libraries. The regulations go with the territory, so there is no alternative except to have at least a general acquaintance with them. More than that, the library administrator may inadvertently be violating one or more of the mandates on the books. For example, are all the requirements met for hiring disabled persons, requirements that have recently been spelled out in federal legislation? The Americans with Disabilities Act of 1992 is quite explicit as to the considerations that should be given to applicants with handicaps. Obviously one cannot hire a person confined to a wheelchair to shelve books, a job that requires standing and reaching and stooping. But what of other positions in the acquisition and cataloging sections, and even at the circulation desk? Can a person in a wheelchair who is otherwise qualified handle such jobs if reasonable adjustment of work space is made?

Perhaps it will help to remember that each of the dictates started originally in the interest of employees, no matter how rigid and confining they may seem at the present time. They reflect social policy, and by and large have been accepted and approved by both the public and the courts. Even civil service had as its purpose the elimination of political and personal favoritism from public employment.

The library personnel administrator has no choice except to walk through this uneven field with care, as through an obstacle course. The following pages will point out some of the mileposts and twists and turns in the path. But it must be remembered that the terrain changes with time, as new legislation is passed and court decisions are rendered. When facing particular issues, from the prospect of a labor union to charges of discrimination, the administrator needs a guide through the labyrinth, in the form of specialized legal counsel.

The public library faces a special legal question. Established in most cases under state statutes, and governed directly by a local board of trustees, the question arises of what independence from local regulations the library has. If the city or town has an affirmative action program, is the library board held to that program? In most cases the library follows such local policies, rather than seeking to exert any legal independence it may have, and for a very practical reason: the bulk of its money comes from the municipality, so it is not disposed to wander outside the local fold. Thus the public library finds itself adhering to local civil service regulations, of which it is usually critical.

Understanding the legal basis of any decision or practice requires (1) acquaintance with the law as passed by legislative bodies, (2) thorough knowledge of the regulations adopted by government bodies to carry out the laws, and (3) more than a passing impression of court cases which examine the constitutionality of the law and the extent to which regulations are consistent with the law. This is a tall order for the public librarian, requiring a definite period of study, and preferably with legal counsel available if needed.

Nor are the school and college libraries excluded from observing the law because they are parts of larger entities. On the contrary, most of these same legal requirements apply to their parent institutions and therefore to them; in addition the institutions themselves may have added to the regulations, thus extending the rules to which the library must conform.

But even knowledge of details of law, regulations and court cases is not enough. Reflected in the laws affecting personnel is the social policy of the nation and the locality, the way that racial and sexual and other policies have been worked out by the body politic. At times the personnel administrator—even in as circumscribed an agency as the library—feels like the arbiter of national policy, a heavy load to carry.

DISCRIMINATION

Let's start with discrimination, a particularly thorny patch in the legal path. The Civil Rights Act of 1964 prohibited discrimination in selection, promotion or dismissal of personnel for reasons of race, color, religion, sex or national origin. Originally this applied only to enterprises engaged in interstate commerce. However, the Equal Opportunity Employment Act of 1972 extended the provisions to educational institutions and agencies of state and local government.

A few characteristics of these laws are worth pointing out. Normally any challenge under the law must come from aggrieved parties, individuals who believe they have been discriminated against. This means that any agency that has not been challenged—such as the library—is not necessarily free of discrimination but simply has not been charged. Originally, as interpreted by the courts, the burden of proof of innocence rested with the accused agency, but more recently this has shifted, putting the burden of proof on the individual or group bringing the charge of discrimination. In general the courts have upheld the legislation, a notable case being Griggs vs. Duke Power, which actually awarded retroactive seniority to an employee who claimed to have been passed over in promotion. Finally, the laws do not limit discrimination to females but apply generally to the sex of employees hired and promoted, which means that charges could be brought concerning prejudice against men—a possibility that libraries may want to note. At least one case is on record of a male library employee passed over for promotion who charged that this was due to sex discrimination.

In general, library administrators believe that they have not discriminated in employment. This is not necessarily true. For example, the practices of the Library of Congress in minority hiring and promotion were brought before a committee of the House of Representatives in 1993, and the Librarian of Congress was told "to either tell his

172 Library Personnel Administration

managers to hire more blacks or tell them we'll find somebody to take their place who can.''[1]

As another example, a news note not long ago reported charges by two employees of the Minneapolis Public Library that they had been passed over for promotion for many years because they are African Americans (Library Hotline, December 7, 1992, p.1). It would be a mistake to assume that libraries are somehow exempt from this problem of possible discrimination.

Now a new twist on sex discrimination appears in the form of homosexuals. Here again cases have appeared in libraries, with lesbians in one instance claiming that insurance coverage should be extended to their domestic partners. The general feeling about homosexuals remains emotional, but no matter what moral judgment is made, discrimination should be avoided here as elsewhere. The sexual orientation of individuals does not affect their ability to perform in library jobs.

All managers with responsibility for personnel should double-check their actions and attitudes for discrimination. Prejudice can become built-in and unconscious, and library administrators are not immune to biases in their culture. How else to account for the evident discrimination in the Library of Congress, which has come to the surface more than once in recent years? Managers must be able to stand aside and avoid prejudices, even if they are endemic in the society. Either that, or the law in time will catch up with them.

While librarians typically would not consider it discrimination, the courts have become involved when individuals have been denied access to libraries. The case of a homeless man in Morristown, New Jersey, has become notorious. The individual was denied access because he troubled other users and he had a foul smell. The man challenged the action with the support of the American Civil Liberties Union in a case that went through several court hearings before being decided in the United States Courts of Appeal.[2]

The administrator is in alien territory among the legislative brambles and should tread carefully.

AFFIRMATIVE ACTION

Laws against discrimination led to the concept of affirmative action under Executive Order 11246. This idea proposes that where definite discrimination in the past can be proven, a plan may be adopted favoring appointment and promotion of minorities (women as well as African-Americans and Hispanics) in order to restore proper balance. This often takes the form of quotas. There has been reaction against this practice, on the grounds that it discriminates against white males. Birmingham, Alabama has had an affirmative action program for a decade which has been challenged by white police officers, fire fighters and other government employees. A recent Federal Court ruling affirmed the plan and concluded that it "did not unnecessarily trammel the rights of whites and did not violate their constitutional rights."[3]

The reaction against favoring minorities has been widespread, and in general is backed by public opinion. A poll in 1993, in answer to the question, "Do you believe that where there has been job discrimination in the past, preference in hiring should be given to blacks today?" only 28% of white respondents were of the opinion that such preference should be given, while 66% of Afro-Americans agreed with the practice.[3]

Libraries have seldom been caught up in this controversy, except indirectly when the hiring practices of a whole governmental jurisdiction have been challenged. In the professional ranks, relatively few African Americans or Hispanics have been attracted to library schools and therefore have not been available for employment. But the issue does apply to non-professional personnel, where libraries are expected to stand against discrimination. The fact that there have been few challenges to date should not make for complacency, because once again it is worth remembering that the issue arises only when incumbents raise a challenge. Every library would be wise to check itself on this matter and to stay ahead of any protests. It is easy, in an institution as traditional and middle-of-the-road as the library, to assume that it is best staffed by members of the majority, an assumption that could be made without due reflection. Then there are public libraries that assume that black staff members should be used in predominantly black neighborhoods and whites in other areas. Is it too much to ask that library administrators be color-blind?

Although libraries have not often been caught up in affirmative action programs, there has been some effort in this direction.[4] Very little progress is reported in increasing the proportion of African Americans either in library schools or on the staffs of libraries. The article cited recommends more cultural diversity in library programs—in collections, in displays, in activities—as a means of showing minorities that libraries would provide a compatible work environment.

Women have been amply represented in the ranks of staff members in librarianship—in fact, it has been seen as a women's profession. Actually, in recent years men have constituted approximately one-quarter of the students in library schools, so that the pool of trained applicants is not evenly balanced. Thus we have the traditional concept of the librarian as a woman, despite the intermingling of men on library staffs. Given these conditions, it is doubtful whether discrimination on sexual grounds could be charged against libraries. In the non-professional and support ranks, women predominate on library staffs, but once again not because of any bias in hiring but because of the make-up of the applicants who seek clerical and related jobs in libraries.

Where discrimination does occur, according to the view of some female librarians, is in the selection of chief librarians in larger libraries. Here there is some predominance of men, particularly in large public libraries. If a sexual bias does play a role at this level, it is the result of decisions not by library administrators but by boards of directors of libraries and of city officials, who in some cases consciously or unconsciously believe that men should run larger enterprises. Certainly the door is not closed to women who aspire to major management positions in libraries, as evidenced by their numbers at the head of both larger academic and public libraries.

Similarly, it would be difficult to sustain a charge of discrimination by libraries on the grounds of race. Minorities have not been attracted to graduate library study in any numbers, so that there are few from which to pick for professional positions. Whether some libraries serving predominantly white user groups would hesitate to hire a black reference librarian is unknown, because the possibility has seldom materialized. When it comes to clerical and support staff, libraries appear to reflect the labor pool from which such workers are selected, with some minority members if that is the make-up of the area. Afro-Americans do serve at service desks and in other capacities in libraries.

Most libraries could properly claim to be equal-opportunity employers. The further step of affirmative action is another matter. Most libraries have not gone out of their way to select minority applicants if they have both black and white prospects with adequate qualifications. Nor have libraries brought in minority members and given them special training so that they could handle available assignments. Not having been discriminatory in hiring practices, most libraries feel little obligation to practice affirmative action.

Personnel administrators must be alert to both the legal and the human requirements for minority hiring and promotion. The Equal Employment Opportunity Act continues in force, and minority members are quick to seek its protection if they sense discrimination. Particularly must this be kept in mind in promotions. It is easy to avoid promoting a qualified black staff member to head of department, on the grounds that white subordinates would not be comfortable in this situation. Race bias is still rife in American society. It should have no place in library personnel practices.

DISABILITIES

The Americans with Disabilities Act of 1992, referred to previously, mentions libraries specifically under Title III

(Public Accommodations) and generally in Title II (Public Service), relating to state and local governments. Librarians have been concerned about proper access to buildings for some time; some libraries have established ramps and other accommodations, others have been uncertain whether action was really necessary. This uncertainty will progressively be removed as applicants and court cases arise under the law in these next few years. Solving the problem can no longer be postponed.

That is, it cannot be postponed unless the administrator decides to seek refuge under the legal provision that building access must be provided if this can be accomplished without undue "difficulty or expense," which presumably will be further clarified as more cases are carried to adjudication. Another provision gives relief if alternation to a building that has been declared of historical significance would do injury to its appearance. Library administrators would be wise not to reach out too quickly to these loopholes, because enforcement is sure to become more stringent. Furthermore, putting off adjustments will still deny access to the handicapped. The problem should be brought to the fore by administrators, and appropriate action taken quickly rather than put off the day.

Proper adjustment applies not only to the entrance to the building but also to accommodations inside. Is elevator service available if there are service facilities or collections on upper or lower floors? Are ramps provided if floors are at different levels? What about adjustment of toilet facilities? In any new construction or additions to a building these factors must definitely be taken into account.

Most significant for the present treatment of personnel, the Disabilities Act specifically applies to hiring and promoting of staff as well as access to the public. Individuals with handicaps are given civil rights protection. If otherwise qualified, applicants with disabilities are not to be denied employment.

This should send personnel administrators back to their job descriptions (see Chapter 4). These should be explicit about physical or visual or hearing requirements for the position under consideration. If a library were to be challenged for passing over a handicapped person, its defense would be that the individual could not handle the position, and it is the job description that would be used to define what the position requires. If the job description did not specify the amount and kind of physical activity involved, the library's case would be definitely weakened. The same line of reasoning applies to reading or communication, which involve sight and hearing. The more complete the job description, the more protected the library.

Once again the legislation leaves a grey area. Employment of a handicapped applicant should be considered if requirements could be met with "reasonable accommodation" and without undue hardship on the part of the employer. What extent of adjustment is reasonable on the part of the library is still to be determined. Presumably this will apply to modifying equipment and the desk or work area, and will also bring in part-time or flexible work schedules adjusted to available transportation or needs for therapy at specified times.

Would a library be required, for instance, to promote to an administrative position an otherwise qualified person who is hard of hearing? The point could be made by the court that equipment is available that increases the volume of sound of the voice of a staff member dealing with the administrator, and the provision of this equipment would not be an undue hardship on the library. We will be hearing more and more of adjustments made by employers in order to conform to the Americans with Disabilities Act.

A new twist has appeared recently. Some employers have limited the insurance coverage accorded to handicapped persons on the grounds that they impose greater risks than average. The courts have generally struck down this practice, even when it applied to individuals who tested HIV-positive and therefore have a potential for the debilitating effects of AIDS.

The lesson of all this is clear. When confronted with the question of whether to hire or promote an otherwise qualified person who is handicapped, management should lean toward accommodation to the individual. This would avoid entanglement with the law and would be in accord with human values and respect for each individual.[5]

CERTIFICATION

Skilled professions have sought to gain recognition under law. This applies not just to doctors, lawyers and dentists but also to engineers, accountants, pharmacists, veterinarians, architects and others. The motive is two fold: to set skilled practitioners apart as a recognized group and to protect the public against unqualified intruders. By and large both professionals and the public have accepted and support the system.

There are three main ways to gain this recognition and protection: licensing, certification and accreditation of training agencies. The distinction between licensing and certification should be noted. The first requires that candidates must obtain a license in order to practice, with state law to enforce the requirement. Certification is usually a voluntary system, with candidates deciding if they will seek approval and libraries deciding whether they will limit themselves to individuals with certificates. Certification usually functions under state law but may be maintained by a professional association. State certification is sometimes mandatory but this has seldom been rigorously enforced. Licensing is the more stringent method, for the individual who practices without holding a license is considered in violation of law.

Of the three alternatives, the library field essentially depends upon accreditation of library schools. This operates through the accrediting operations of the American Library Association. The Association has not rejected certification but does not depend upon it. Libraries typically specify graduation from an approved program as a prerequisite to professional employment and only occasionally refer to state accreditation listing.

The academic branch of ALA has taken an additional step. In the 1989 ACRL Statement on the Certification and Licensing of Academic Librarians, the requirement of a master's degree from an ALA-accredited program is reaffirmed; it goes on to say that ". . . it opposes certification and licensing in lieu of that degree for academic librarians, either by state agencies or by state or local professional associations."[6]

The situation is different for school librarians, who are involved in the labyrinth of certification of teachers. These extended regulations are promulgated by state education authorities, which also provide enforcement. Teachers must meet certification requirements, and the school librarian or school media specialist is usually included with them. The requirements have often become fairly complicated. In New York State, for example, the school media specialist must show 36 semester hours of library and media courses and 12 hours in education for a provisional certificate valid for five years, and then for a permanent certificate must have a master's degree and 15 hours of social and behavioral science. Over the years such requirements have grown more extensive and more complicated in most states. In some instances they include a teaching certificate and teaching experience in addition to the library requirements. ALA also works with the National Council for the Accreditation of Teacher Education (NCATE) on recognition of school library media specialists.

Sometimes in reform efforts to bring additional people into the teaching ranks, proposals have been made to remove or waive the considerable requirements in order to attract otherwise highly-qualified college graduates. Recently the question has been raised of waiving the requirements for school media specialists, in New York State[7] and elsewhere, but here the motive is to open the door to part-time staffing of the school library or designating a teacher as part-time librarian. This is a step backward, prompted by pressures on educational budgets.

Certification provisions for librarians have accumulated in many states but the movement has slowed down in recent years. The requirements differ from state to state, making for a patchwork and erecting barriers against shifting from state to state. This has led to proposals for a national certification program, presumably administered by the American Library Association, but the Association is not disposed to take on either this project or the national licensing of librarians.

The weight of responsibility for marking off the library profession and for protecting users against substandard performance therefore rests on the ALA program for accrediting library schools. By and large the volunteer accrediting committees have done a conscientious job, although the list of approved schools shows a considerable difference in quality. Noting the frequency with which library schools are criticized in the literature by members of the profession, one cannot help but wonder about the standards that have been used for approval.

MLS DEGREE

A few words should be included about the Master of Library Science (MLS) degree, which has become a fairly standard requirement for professional employment in libraries.

One of the aims behind the various laws relating to employment has been that of removing marginal or nonessential requirements that stand in the way of job applicants. It has been argued that excessive and extraneous requirements discriminate against individuals who would be capable of handling positions, and particularly that they are used to block out members of minorities who cannot obtain the specified requirements because of lack of money.

Protests from excluded groups have identified specific educational requisites in this category—a master's degree, for example. Responding to such protests, governmental units, including the federal civil service, have also raised questions about the MLS requirement.

Librarians have responded that the advanced degree is not only desirable but essential to performing professional duties. This position might take some defending. It would be necessary to show not only that the graduate professional study was appropriate to library service, but beyond that, that it was the only way to become qualified. When we traced the emergence of the professional librarian in an earlier chapter, we raised questions as to whether some years of experience in a library or a subject master's degree would prepare a person for a reference or cataloging or bibliographic position. It would probably be possible to locate instances of individuals performing professional services, and performing them adequately, without the library degree.

And finally, it would be incumbent to show that the necessary body of knowledge could not be obtained at the undergraduate level, assuming that reasonable adjustment could be made in college curricula. This last defense might be particularly difficult to establish because for some years library training was included within the bachelor's degree; more and more technical training in other fields is being included in college curricula in recent years, so library courses in the undergraduate years are not beyond possibility. It is that additional year of graduate study that often stands in the way of college graduates who consider a library career, since it constitutes another financial hurdle that most be overcome.

Certainly educational requirements have been applied to various activities of some complexity, from nursing to engineering, from teaching to accountancy. Schools, colleges and universities have been developed to prepare qualified personnel for such services, and society has been protected by the graduating standards of such institutions. One would hesitate to go to a dentist who had not gone to dental school.

But, as we have seen, librarianship is often misunderstood and devalued by the general public, and indeed also by university authorities. Challenges to the MLS requirement will occur again and librarians should be prepared for it. The defense will be the stronger if graduate librarians engage only in professional duties and if the pursuit of a distinctive body of principles is intensified by library-school faculty members and other researchers in the field. The case for graduate study would be strengthened if library education were based on distinctive theory rather than on technical training in established practices.

The hiring of MLS graduates can be expected to continue. Frankly, one reason is that it does not cost much more to do so than to promote an experienced non-professional. The average beginning salary of graduates is still running under $25,000 a year, which is not much above what would be necessary for a non-graduate veteran on the staff, and less than could be obtained by master's graduates in such fields as science and engineering.

The MLS degree is not a legal requirement imposed from the outside but more a standard which library administrators themselves have adopted, with the cooperation and encouragement of the American Library Association. They can be expected to continue applying the standard, but, as pressures of budgets increase, some agencies will decide to promote their more experienced and capable sub-professionals, and others will recruit some of the best of local college graduates. If such were to occur, few users of libraries would be likely to protest.

Apart from possible outside challenges to the MLS degree, the profession itself should consider whether the graduate library program as it now stands is what is needed for the period ahead. Are the library schools preparing people for the coming stage of electronic communication? Are they helping students to prepare not only for the new period but also pointing out how graduates can advance and control this development? Many library schools have the term Information Science in their title, but the science which they claim is still to be defined and developed. The training now being provided for the MLS degree may be outmoded before current graduates move into senior positions twenty years hence.

UNIONIZATION

Over the years, employee unions have made a contribution to labor relations. Unions have improved salaries in industry and thus added to the standard of living of workers, and they have reduced dangerous and unhealthy working conditions. In recent years unionization in general has not increased—in fact, has decreased in some sectors—in part because salaries and working conditions have become somewhat more advantageous without organized employee action, and in part because governmental regulation has addressed many of the problems of employees (minimum wages, safety, discrimination). Given the economic recession of the last few years some unions have become more negative and protectionist rather than positive in their demands, seeking to hold on to their past gains and to preserve the jobs of individuals who are now members. They have been willing to compromise on wage demands in order to prevent industries from closing or moving.

Business and industrial officials have generally opposed unionization or at least looked upon the movement with skepticism, because this limits management prerogatives. Requests for higher wages and for improved working conditions can threaten the basic goal of profits, and strikes can bring operations to a halt. The prevailing situation is kind of a stand-off, without much gain on either side.

Besides the effect on the bottom line, managers generally have opposed unions because they limit their sovereignty, result in a blurring of authority, provide a convenient mechanism for trouble makers, and make demands on time and energy. Most managers, including library managers, would like to avoid unions.

Much of the approved relationship between employers and employee unions has been formalized in federal law, supplemented by state statutes. The basis for unionization goes back to the "Wagner Act" (The National Industrial Recovery Act of 1933). This was supplemented by the "Taft-Hartley Act" (The Labor- Management Relations Act of 1947) and the Landrum-Griffin amendments of 1959, which put restrictions on the actions of both employers and unions.

Unionization came later to the public and service sectors, really getting underway after World War II. Inroads on libraries came slowly. Several factors mitigate against unionization among librarians: an attitude that unions are not compatible with a white-collar professional enterprise, the fact that few librarians work under conditions that are dangerous and threatening to health, and a gradual improvement in personnel administration in libraries.

Unions do exist in libraries; in fact, a few go back to the 1930s and 1940s. Originally, they functioned primarily in large public libraries for the non-professional rather than the professional staff members but now are found in academic libraries also and cover both professional and non-professional staff members. An analysis of the issues brought forth by the groups found three to predominate: salaries, fringe benefits and grievance procedures.[9]

For affiliation, the American Federation of State, County and Municipal Employees has been turned to by the public library staffs, and teacher groups by school personnel. The American Association of University Professors serves many academic libraries. Strikes have occasionally been called against libraries even though this raises an additional legal issue in governmental jurisdictions. While an increase in unionization in libraries does not appear likely at this stage, the pressure on budgets could revive this interest. Personnel administrators would be wise to keep this prospect in view.

Staff associations within libraries vary from passive social groups to aggressive proponents of employee interests. In a few cases they have served as bargaining agents. Obviously they lack the strength that may come from affiliation with a labor union and the protection of laws giving rights to unions. But, like formal unions, staff associations may provide a vehicle for staff participation in library affairs, and positive administration might well encourage them for this purpose. The effectiveness of the relationship depends on a confident yet empathetic outlook among personnel administrators and active yet responsible leadership from the staff side.

Because of the maze of legislation that applies to relations with unions, personnel administrators in affected libraries need outside help. Close and competent legal counsel is needed at each phase, during the organizing period, negotiating the first contract, in collective bargaining disputes, and in dealing with grievances. This requires more than a general counsel connected with the library (perhaps on the board of directors) and calls for a specialist in labor relations.

Interestingly enough, union negotiations in libraries have included such matters as staff participation in decision-making, career structures, and effective communication between staff and management. Thus the existence of a union can actually be used to further some of the tenets of personnel administration espoused in this volume.

Positive and open personnel administration usually forestalls the growth of union sentiment. If wages and personnel practices and changes in program are developed with staff participation, a reasonable accommodation can be worked out without resorting to formal collective bargaining and union organization.[10]

LIVING WITH THE LAW

Dealing with legal matters and legal restraints need not be an onerous burden on library administrators. Most of the prescriptions in law have come about because authoritarian managers in various instances have violated human interests and human rights, have been challenged by workers, and legislators and courts have acted to protect individuals. Opposition from management has occurred because worker demands can threaten profits.

Library managers, of course, do not have this responsibility for profits. Their concern, their bottom line, is improved service at the point of staff-user contact, and this is fostered by developing motivated librarians using their inner drive to perform and perform well. With this invaluable resource, and with human values to the fore, library personnel administrators are not likely to run afoul of the law. Indeed, where this does happen, one would be well advised to look at the quality of administration as well as the peculiarities of legal prescriptions. Put differently, positive administration is likely also to be legal administration.

REFERENCES

1. "LC minority policies come under attack at House hearings,"*American Libraries* (May 1993): 366.
2. For several articles on this case, see *New Jersey Libraries,* Vol. 25 no. 4. Fall, 1992.
3. *New York Times,* August 18, 1992, A12.
4. *New York Times,* April 4, 1993, Section 1, 12.
5. Cliff Glaviano, and R. Errol Lam, "Academic Libraries and Affirmative Action; Approaching Cultural Diversity in the 1990s," *College and Research Libraries* Vol. 51, No. 6 (1992), 513–523.
6. Donald D. Foos, and Nancy C. Pack, eds. *How Libraries Must Comply with the Americans with Disabilities Act* (Phoenix, AZ: Oryx, 1992).
7. *College and Research Library News,* Vol. 50, No. 10 (November 1989), 893.
8. B. Goldberg, "New York Governor Proposes Lifting School Library Mandate," *American Libraries,* 24 (March 1993), 206.
9. John W. Weatherford, *Librarians' Agreements: Bargaining for a Heterogeneous Profession* (Metuchen, N.J.: Scarecrow Press, 1988).
10. Theodore L. Guyton, *Unionization: The Viewpoint of Librarians* (Chicago: American Library Association, 1975), 40.

10. FUTURE OF PERSONNEL ADMINISTRATION

We have seen that libraries, for all their positive service programs and their relatively humane personnel systems, are not well adapted to change, particularly to basic change that may alter not just their methods but also their very goals and functions. Yet we are entering a period of profound development in two technologies that directly impact libraries: Computerized recording and access to information, whether the datum of fact or the volume of exposition, and electronic communication that transfers material from central reservoirs to individual screens. No one can say just how far these trends will move and what effect they will have on the public and on institutions. But it is clear that we are moving toward the electronic library in some form.

Currently the newspapers are making much of the joining of computers with television to open interchange between the home and sources of entertainment. The family will be able to choose readily among 500 channels, visit the shopping mall, and even change the angle from which they can see a baseball game. This is to be the age of the empowered couch potato.

As a kind of afterthought, access in the home to libraries at a distance is thrown into the hopper. But this will not occur until the contents of libraries are machine-readable and until libraries are connected to the airwaves, both of which are conceivable in the coming period. The computerized catalog of holdings is ready for this, as also are a variety of data sources, and even a few reference books in suitable form. This, of course, is only a small part of the library collection, but conversion of text to digital interactive form is somewhere down the road. And, as in all basic changes, libraries will need personnel prepared and eager to participate in this revolution. It is because most agencies are not ready in this respect that the participation of libraries in this next stage is problematical. We come back to the proposition that personnel is all.

Overall, these two trends of augmented computerization and electronic communication will have a decided social and economic effect, similar to technological change in the past. To gain perspective, it is worth reminding ourselves of a few of these critical periods. The opening up of steam railroads in the country in the 1880s and 1890s, the widespread acceptance of the automobile in the 1920s, and the spread of computerization in the 1970s are examples (the dates of course refer not to the original inventions but to their widespread application and acceptance). The next impact will come from electronic communication shortly after the year 2000.

The revolution is not just in prospect; it is already underway. New technology comes at us from every side: personal computers, CD-Roms, interactive video, parallel processing, coupled with the uses to which these innovations have been put—on-line data bases, facsimile transmission, communications networks, desk-top publishing. Already in place is a network in the special field of science, Internet, which serves scientists around the world, bringing information immediately without the delay of publication in a journal. "It's the most fundamental shift since Gutenberg."[1]

Both government and business are getting into the act. The present federal government puts what it calls the "Information Super-Highway" at the forefront of its economic agenda. Federal research grants are now in place to increase traffic on the super-highway. A consolidation has occurred between U.S. West (telephone) and Time-Warner to bring individual choice of both entertainment and information directly into the home. Macy's Department Store is taking to the air. The revolution gathers speed.

WHERE LIBRARIES ARE

Libraries are only part-way down this road at present. At least three stages or phases in utilization of new computer technology can be discerned:

1. Machine-readable records as an aid in carrying out traditional library functions and record-keeping
2. Computerized data bases as supplements to printed reference materials
3. Computer-based records of text as a substitute or re-placement for printed resources—the electronic library

Most libraries have moved, somewhat gingerly, into the first stage. Circulation records have been automated. The card catalog is being replaced by the computerized record. Periodical indexes are being combined into a single data base. As a second step, the proliferating information data bases—Dialog, Medline, Business Dateline, Internet, etc.—are being subscribed to as budgets permit. In each case new technology is helping the library do what it has long done by manual methods.

Users are properly impressed when, asking if they still have books out in circulation, they are informed from information on a screen that all their borrowings have been returned but the record shows that they still owe thirty cents in overdue fines. Users are more impressed when they go to the catalog for a subject search and are given many more leads than were possible in the old card catalog. The library is simply doing more rapidly and more thoroughly what it has done from time immemorial. Personnel have had to adjust, but once they get the hang of the new techniques, they settle in and in most cases produce more than before.

Users are likely to be even more impressed when they seek information in the library—on a chemical formula, on an obscure disease, on new corporate stock, on a minor figure in history—and discover that they have access to data kept far outside the library walls. Data bases are proliferating, covering more and more topics and interests, a kind of new form of collection, scattered at a distance but electronically accessible to any subscriber. The data bases were not made by libraries, nor are they maintained by the usual library staff. They can be likened to a utility available to the library for a fee, a utility that extends the reach of the agency.

The third stage of development of computer-based materials opens more far-reaching prospects. It is helpful to back away a bit to sense their full import.

THE ELECTRONIC LIBRARY

For centuries both scholars and general readers have depended on written-printed sources, in book, pamphlet and journal form. While a small selection of these could be purchased and kept right at hand in the home, office and classroom, the larger collections were gathered and organized in libraries. The user went to the collection available in the community, the school, the university, the business firm or the special-purpose institution.

Increasingly the material in these collections is becoming available in machine-readable form. This started with bibliographies and indexes to journals, and then moved on to the contents of the journals themselves. Information data bases have been assembled in this form. Currently whole encyclopedias and whole books are beginning to become available electronically. In ten years this last development will have progressed much further, and will be given a push forward when fiber-optic cable becomes more widely available and when telephone companies and cable companies combine.

Of course the remarkable thing about this whole trend is that users do not have to go to the library to gain access to resources—if they have the proper equipment. What is needed can be called up on the computer screen, whether a datum of information or a whole page.

There will be cost involved for the viewer, just as there is cost in maintaining a large library in the home. Appropriate computer capacity is necessary, probably with a printer attachment. Then there will be a charge for access to the service, as there is a charge for cable today. Experimental programs now underway are designed primarily to find out how many people will be prepared to make the financial outlay.

The skeptic quite probably says that many people will still prefer to stay with the book. Exactly so, which will result in present libraries becoming the back-up book source to electronic materials, even as the latter are back-ups to large collections of print at present. But it must be remembered that the machine-readable material can still end up in printed form right at the desk of the individual user, assuming that person has a desk-top printer. In this case, convenience of access will be greatly enhanced, and convenience has been a key factor in the growth of everything from shopping (all together under one roof in the mall) to television (theater and concert hall and athletic field right in the house).

What will be the mission of the library in the year 2010? Perhaps as the auxiliary book collection, searched out by the portion of readers who want the printed page. Or perhaps as electronic collections with a whole range of computerized resources, beyond what individual users can afford to subscribe to, even as today they cannot afford to buy all the books they might need.

In the latter case—that is, libraries assuming a greater role—two somewhat different lines of development can be envisioned. In one alternative, libraries would become fewer in number (smaller agencies in schools, colleges and towns cutting back and becoming limited working collections) and those that remain becoming much larger in size and standing behind the lesser agencies. The user would go on up the ladder to the stronger centers as necessary, or materials would be transferred temporarily from the center to the lesser agency. To a degree this is the pattern that has evolved naturally over the years and it may progress further in the future.

The other alternative is for existing collections to be coordinated into a joint unit by means of union catalogs which provide identification and location of all holdings in a region, with access gained by electronic communication. The closest we come to this pattern at present is in the 3R's (Reference and Research Resources) program in New York State. The 3R's are coordinating units standing above individual libraries and systems of libraries, a level below the State Library but above the various service outlets. Each serves a region, nine in all over the State. They have built up union catalogs and union indexes for present holdings and encourage access either by old-fashioned delivery or by facsimile transmission. As yet the computerized union records do not include text, but this is down the road a distance. The 3R's system is financed primarily by the State. They can be said to represent one step into the future.

And where will such development leave the individual librarian? This depends on how much libraries move into the new prospect. If libraries hold back and stay about where they are, the librarian will have much the present role, the gatherer and organizer of the collection in printed form and the guide to those who hold to the traditional book—but on a lesser scale because the relative use of books for information and text will be smaller. Or, if the agency increasingly becomes the access point to computerized information, the librarian will become the keeper of the data base rather than the keeper of the book. If recorded knowledge in whatever form becomes the province of the library, the librarian could become the coordinator of the new information age.

If we are to have information and text super-highways, who will plan out the routes and decide on the connections? Who will prepare the maps needed for this new territory? Who will serve as the American Automobile Association to the information super-highways, planning out routes for travelers?

This could become the role of the librarian, the specialist in designing information and text networks and in guiding searchers in their use. If so, the public image of the librarian would be different from the present one and the remuneration would no longer be at the bottom of the professional scale. Either that or librarians will be pushed into the backflow while other agencies function in the mainstream.

Role of the Administrator

If the bright prospect is to be grasped, change will have to occur at three levels within libraries: the front office, the supervisor on the line, and the individual worker.

Library directors can either look back, seeking to preserve the strength that libraries have achieved, or look ahead, seeking to prepare for a changed role in the period ahead. Of the two, the look back is easier and more natural. Most chief librarians would in time retire, feeling that their ministration had been worthy and successful if their agency was doing what it did when they came into office, and perhaps doing more of it and at a higher level. The look the other way, into the uncertain future, is more problematical and hazardous. What if one seeks to lead toward the future and finds when one gets there that another institution has grown up to control and guide the use of computerized knowledge? What if the leader sees a promising road ahead but the staff refuses to follow? Most chief administrators will choose the easier course, but what will happen to libraries will depend on whether a minority of leaders will step out and find the new role for their institutions. This is how progress has ever occurred, when Henry Ford decided to build an assembly line, when Jonas Salk developed the polio vaccine, when Robert Goddard designed the first rocket.

It is encouraging to note occasional efforts within the profession to look forward in detail into the next period. One example is in the field of serials, where a group of librarians is preparing for the age of networked information.[2]

Will the leaders be lucky enough to have personnel administrators and supervisors who will inculcate acceptance of change in the staff? Once again it will be a chancy game, but some supervisors will catch the vision and be challenged by it. Then their full skill as facilitators will be called on. Staff will have to be assured that they will not lose their jobs, will have to be motivated, taught new skills, counseled when frustrations occur, and rewarded when they respond.

The multiple skills of the personnel administrator are needed to maintain and improve quality in present libraries. Even more they are needed if libraries are to respond to the heady challenge of the coming century. Will professional librarians go along into this new age? Will uncertainty about what they will be called on to do and doubt about whether they will even have a job cause them to hold fast in the safe haven of the established library?

The answer depends on the kind of personnel administration that will prevail in the next years. The supervisor should not try to paint a golden picture of the library in the 21st century. No one sees that picture clearly and painting it in bright colors may repel rather than attract the people at the service desks. The institution will go step-by-step into the future, and staff at best can be expected to go along step-by-step. At the outset, management—to the extent that is honest and likely—should reassure staff that they have a place in the new order, that their employment will be assured. Personnel administrators should introduce each of the prospects just ahead, carefully and thoroughly, so that librarians can feel confident in each of them. Training in use of each new tool should be thorough, so that staff members feel that they have control. Even for professionals this will mean re-training, just as the physician needs re-training from time to time. The overall gain being achieved should be made clear, not just the value of the individual technique.

In other words, personnel administration at its best will need to be practiced. Somehow we cannot get away from the key role of people facilitation as the road to progress.

The methods expounded in this volume will be called on at every turn. The personnel administrator, at every step, must remember the basics:

- know and communicate the advantages
- communicate early and thoroughly
- reassure as to job security
- get staff input—but stay in charge

  - involve the critics—answer the concerns
  - give time for staff to discuss and absorb

You are the facilitator, not the dictator. Will staff members respond? Remember that many are seeking a sense of achievement in their jobs. There is satisfaction in being at the forefront of a movement. There is a reward in the admiration of family and friends. It will be an exciting and rewarding time. Propitiate with those who hold back, commiserate with those about to retire from the ranks, for both will miss the challenge.

For those who go along on the journey, this could be an exciting period, similar to the stimulus in Silicon Valley as computers came into their own in the 1970s and 1980s. The financial rewards will probably not be the same but the sense of accomplishment could be as great.

Note that these changes will occur within the working life of librarians now on the job, certainly within the next twenty years. It is not too soon to have these prospects in mind in building and maintaining library staffs. Nor is it too soon to review goals and objectives in anticipation of evolution that will occur whether librarians wish it or not.

ENDURING TRAITS

What will not change in the period ahead are the abilities and characteristics needed by effective personnel administrators that have been reviewed in this volume. It is worth listing these traits here at the end:

  - dedication to purpose and a sense of direction
  - initiative in starting action
  - follow-through in getting things done
  - empathy in sensing the viewpoint and reaction of staff
  - communication skills in dealing with people of different backgrounds
  - judgment in analyzing situations
  - skill in planning and organizing work
  - willingness to consider change and venture into the unknown

And what can only be called character, made up of such traits as integrity, fairness and consistency.

Libraries—and librarians—now enter a period that calls for new leadership, which must be derived from age-old qualities that have always marked the individual who will venture into darkness or climb the long hill.

REFERENCES

1. *New York Times*, May 18, 1993, C1.
2. Suzanne McMahon, Miriam Palne, and Pamela Dunn, *If We Build It; Scholarly Communication and Networking Technologies* (Binghamton, NY: Haworth Press), 1993.

BIBLIOGRAPHY

This is a selected list. Not one title has been included simply because it has to do with personnel. Without exception, every one of these books and articles will add to the administrator's ability to develop personnel. Some are older, going back to the foundation of human relations in administration, while others are current, for instance about Japanese methods. Even the items pertaining just to one type of library—public, school, or academic—have something of value for personnel administrators. Think of this bibliography more as a professional reading list, to be used as a reading program over a period of time.

Argyris, Chris. *Integrating the Individual and the Organization.* New York: Wiley, 1964.

Association of Research Libraries. *Changing Role of the ARL Library Personnel Officer.* Washington: ARL Systems and Procedures Exchange Center, 1978.

Association of Research Libraries. *Performance Appraisal in ARL Libraries.* Washington: ARL Systems and Procedures Exchange Center, 1979.

Barnard, Chester. *The Functions of the Executive.* Cambridge, MA: Harvard University Press, 1968.

Beach, Dale S. *Personnel: the Management of People at Work.* New York: Macmillan, 1980.

Cascis, Wayne F. *Managing Human Resources; Productivity, Quality of Work Life, Profits.* New York: McGraw-Hill, 1989.

Cowley, John. *Personnel Management in Libraries.* Hamden, CT: Bingley, 1982.

Creth, Sheila and Duda, F., eds. *Personnel Administration in Libraries.* New York: Neal-Schuman, 1989.

De Prospo, Ernest R. "Personnel Evaluation as an Impetus to Growth," *Library Trends* 20 (July, 1971), 60–70.

Drucker, Peter F. *Managing the Non-Profit Organization; Practices and Principles.* New York: HarperCollins, 1990.

Drucker, Peter F. *Post-Capitalist Society.* New York: Harper, 1993.

Duda, F. "Columbia's Two-Track System of Professional Ranks and Position Categories," *College and Research Libraries* 4 (July, 1980), 295–304.

Haimann, Theodore and Hilgert, Raymond L. *Supervision; Concepts and Practices of Management.* Cincinnati: Southwestern, 1972.

Heim, Kathleen M. "Toward a Work-Force Analysis of the School Library Media Professional," *School Media Quarterly* 9 (Summer, 1981), 235–249.

Herzberg, Frederick. *Work and the Nature of Man.* Cleveland: World Publishing, 1966.

Hilton, R.C. "Performance Evaluation of Library Personnel," *Special Libraries* 69 (November, 1978), 429–434.

Hunsaker, Phillip L. *The Art of Managing People.* Englewood Cliffs, NJ: Prentice-Hall, 1980.

Kroll, H.R. "Beyond Evaluation: Performance Appraisal as a Planning and Motivational Tool in Libraries," *Journal of Academic Librarianship* 5(January, 1980), 329–334.

Likert, Rensis. *The Human Organization; Its Management and Value.* New York: McGraw-Hill, 1967.

McGregor, Douglas. *The Human Side of Enterprise.* New York: McGraw-Hill, 1960.

Maloney, R.K.M., ed. *Personnel Development in Libraries.* New Brunswick, NJ: Rutgers University, 1977.

Martin, Lowell A., ed. *Personnel Administration in Libraries.* Chicago: University of Chicago Press, 1945.

Martin, Murray S. *Issues in Personnel Management in Academic Libraries.* Greenwich, CT: JAI Press, 1981.

Maslow, Abraham. *Motivation and Personality.* New York: Harper & Row, 1954.

Metcalf, Henry C. and Urwick, L. eds. *Dynamic Administration: the Papers of Mary Parker Follett.* New York: Harper, 1941.

Ouchi, William. *Theory Z; How American Business Can Meet the Japanese Challenge.* Reading, PA: Addison-Wesley, 1981.

Ozaki, Robert. *Human Capitalism.* Tokyo: Kodausha International, 1991.

Parkinson, C. Northcote. *Parkinson's Law and Other Studies in Administration.* Boston: Houghton-Mifflin, 1957.

Peter, Laurence J. *The Peter Principle.* New York: Morrow, 1969.

Pigors, Paul J. *Personnel Administration.* New York: McGraw-Hill, 1981.

Ricking, Myrl and Booth, Robert E. *Personnel Utilization in Libraries; a Systems Approach.* Chicago: American Library Association, 1974.

Sullivan, Peggy and Ptacek, William. *Public Libraries: Smart Practices in Personnel.* Littleton, CO: Libraries Unlimited, 1982.

White, Herbert S. *Library Personnel Management.* White Plains, NY: Knowledge Industry Publications, 1985.

Yoder, Dale. *Personnel Principles and Policies; Modern Manpower Management.* Englewood Cliffs, NJ: Prentice-Hall, 1960.

INDEX

ABOUT THE AUTHOR

Lowell A. Martin (B.S., Illinois Institute of Technology, Ph.D., University of Chicago) has worked in libraries, library schools and in publishing where he has had responsibility for personnel. Branch Librarian and Assistant to the Chief Librarian, Chicago Public Library, Professor and Associate Dean, School of Library Service, Columbia University, and organizer and Dean of the library school at Rutgers University. For 10 years Dr. Martin was Vice President of Grolier Incorporated, where he had responsibility for 800 editorial workers. In recent years he has conducted administrative surveys of several city libraries, in Chicago, Los Angeles, San Francisco, Atlanta, Dallas, Philadelphia, Baltimore and Memphis. Author of *Library Response to Urban Change* (American Library Association, 1969) and *Organizational Structure of Libraries* (Scarecrow, 1984).